# PRAYING THE BOOK
## OF REVELATION

Elmer L. Towns

**Destiny Image® Publishers, Inc.**
**P.O. Box 310**
**Shippensburg, PA 17257-0310**

*"Speaking to the Purposes of God for this Generation*
*and for the Generations to Come."*

For Worldwide Distribution, Printed in the U.S.A.

ISBN 10: 0-7684-2420-8

ISBN 13: 978-0-7684-2420-1

This book and all other Destiny Image, Revival Press, MercyPlace, Fresh Bread, Destiny Image Fiction, and Treasure House books are available at Christian bookstores and distributors worldwide.

1 2 3 4 5 6 7 8 9 10 11 / 09 08 07

For a U.S. bookstore nearest you, call
**1-800-722-6774.**

For more information on foreign distributors, call
**717-532-3040.**

Or reach us on the Internet:
**www.destinyimage.com**

# CONTENTS

SECTION TEN

# PREFACE

I want you to do more than read the Scriptures; I want you to pray the Scriptures. Why? Praying is a heart response to God, while reading the Bible is usually a head response to Him. Therefore, pray the Scriptures with all your heart so that you will believe...love...yield...and worship God.

*Praying the Book of Revelation* is one volume in a series that has covered several years. You should first read the other three books in this series:

*Praying the Psalms*

*Praying Proverbs, Ecclesiastes, and Song of Solomon*

*Praying the Book of Job.*

Then, notice the planned releases listed at the end of this volume.

When writing this series, I first translated the Greek (New Testament) and Hebrew (Old Testament) into modern day English. This is not an exact word for word translation, but an "idea for idea" equivalency. Next, I transposed the text into the second person so that the reader talks to God using the personal "You." Of course, I added some other prayers for you to pray as you cover each chapter. Also in this volume, *Praying the Book of Revelation*, I've included historical background, geography, and explanations to help you better understand the message of Revelation. This is not an inspired version of Scripture, but a human paraphrase. So, read your Bible along with praying the Scriptures.

May God open your eyes as you read *Praying the Book of Revelation*, and may you know Christ better. Then, let's pray with John, *"Even so come, Lord Jesus."*

Sincerely yours in Christ,
Elmer Towns
Written at my home at the foot of the Blue Ridge Mountains
Fall 2006

# FOREWORD

As the wife of the author, Elmer Towns, I consider myself an unusual person to write an introduction for this book. But I have some unusual things to share with you about this book and my husband.

As he was recuperating from cancer surgery, he began translating the Book of Revelation into prayers while writing the accompanying story of John. I didn't get particularly excited about this project because Elmer has written over 100 books (see www.elmertowns.com) in his lifetime, and I've read all of them in their rough drafts. I thought this was just another one of his projects.

But as I began reading *Praying the Book of Revelation*, I started to weep. I felt I was in the presence of frail John, weakened by age and imprisonment. This time, my husband had captured something that he had not previously put on paper. Because of Elmer's weakened condition after three and a half hours of surgery, he felt John's pain and was able to relay those feelings in writing.

I became so choked up that I couldn't finish the first chapter; I had to lay the manuscript aside and begin to pray and worship God. My prayer is that readers will experience worship as I did at that moment.

There's an additional theme that this book explores—impending death. John wrote the Book of Revelation knowing he would soon die. After surgery—and other conditions—Elmer's pain was so intense that he honestly thought he would die. He even prayed that he was willing to die if that is where his pain would lead. This manuscript captures the experience of facing death, both by John and the martyrs described in Revelation. Today Elmer is as healthy as ever and there's no sign of cancer...Amen!

In conclusion, it is important to note that Elmer led a study group to Greece and Turkey and visited the cave on the Isle of Patmos where John wrote the Book of Revelation. When Elmer mentions in this book that the cave is "black stone," "cold and damp," and "only ten brisk steps from one wall...to the other," he knows these facts firsthand because he was actually there and stepped off the cave's dimensions. Outside the cave is a natural amphitheatre where the prisoners prayed for John as he was writing the Revelation. It was there also that Elmer preached from Revelation chapter 1 to approximately 100 people on Easter Sunday, 2005.

My prayer is that you will experience the message of this book as I did when I first read it. Then, may we all look forward to the return of Christ.

—Ruth Towns
Wife of Elmer Towns for 53 years
Fall 2006

# Section One

# WORSHIP:
## WHEN YOU COME TO THE END

### Scripture: Revelation 1:1-20

The old man's tired eyes popped open, but he didn't move his head. There was a faint light at the mouth of the cave. His ancient body had a terminal ache; he knew death was close. He was almost 100 years old. But he was not expecting to leave this life by death—he was expecting Jesus to return. His weary eyes crinkled as his young heart prayed…

"Even so come, Lord Jesus…"

Sleeping on the damp, black, rock floor of the cave chilled his bones, but it was better than sleeping outside where the wet dew of Heaven gave him the flu. The inmates who were his parishioners—those he had won to Christianity—insisted he sleep in the cave.

*Today is Sunday*, the old man thought while trying to blow the cobwebs out of his mind. *Today, I will preach to my flock.*

The cave was cut out of Mt. Elias, a ragged rock that reaches 800 feet out of the Aegean Sea, the highest peak on the small Isle of Patmos. The Roman Caesar Domitian had chosen this isolated bastion during the 14th year of his reign as the home for political prisoners. Then he sent John the apostle to Patmos in an attempt to destroy Christianity. The arrest papers delivered to the guards along with John charged him with treason, "Testifying that Jesus Christ is King and preaching the Word of God."

Yet, this tiny island—ten miles long and six miles wide—could not imprison a person whom Christ had set free. Consequently, aged John had never feared the island, nor had he ever felt isolated. He was over 90 years of age when he first came to Patmos and had walked with Christ

PRAYING THE BOOK OF REVELATION

ever since he had left his fishing nets to follow the Master. He was not alone on Patmos—Jesus was with him; the Lord Jesus lived in his heart.

"Don't come to get me for the sermon," John told Ansel, the young assistant who was bringing him a cup of water and morsel of bread. Ansel had a large frame that once had been muscular, but now, his was an emaciated body covered by taut skin. The meager rations on Patmos barely kept life and limb together. He had been chosen by the others to protect John because he was the strongest, and also the meekest with the heart of a servant. The young man quietly put a cup of water on the crude table, then covered a scrap of bread with a clean cloth. Even in the cave there were flies. Old John told his assistant, "God is calling me to pray...don't disturb me. I will come preach when I finish praying...."

Each Sunday, the converts would gather in the amphitheater in front of the cave, waiting for John to emerge. Protected by the rocks from the ocean's wind, John would sit in a chair to preach to his church of prisoners—free from sin, but prisoners of Christ.

And while the church waited patiently for John each Sunday morning, they also knelt in prayer, asking God to give John a message for them. While they waited for a sermon, they were interceding to God. Sometimes their wait was short, and at other times it was long; but no one minded. The longer they waited, the more God had to say to them through the apostle John.

"Don't disturb me," John repeated his instructions to the young Ansel leaving the cave. "When the Lord tells me what to say," there was a twinkle in his eye, "I'll come out of the cave. But don't come for me until the Lord finishes talking to me."

The prisoners revered John, knowing he was the last of the 12 disciples left alive who had followed Jesus. He had also been the youngest of the 12, and the one whom Jesus especially loved—he had leaned on the Lord's breast. When Jesus had been betrayed, all the other disciples had run away—but not John. He had remained faithful during the trials and was standing at the foot of the cross when he had heard Jesus tell him to take care of Mary, His mother. John had also been the first disciple to go to the tomb on Easter Sunday morning.

Interestingly, all the other disciples who had run away from the dangers of the cross and who had been been afraid of dying, eventually died violent martyrs' deaths. The Christians on Patmos believed the tradition that John would die a natural death, however. Christians all over the Mediterranean world believed it. No Roman emperor would kill him.

The young attendant emerged from the cave to inform the praying prisoners, "John is alive and awake!"

"Amen!" they all cried, grateful that John had not died in his sleep. Their beloved pastor would live another Sunday to preach to them.

All week long, John had been fasting and praying for God to give him a message to preach. God had burdened his heart as he waited in the presence of God...worshiping God...fellowshipping with God...waiting for a special message from God.

John, rising earlier than usual and feeling younger than the age of his ancient body, didn't pick up the cup of water awaiting him on the crude wooden table, nor did he lift the clean white cloth covering the bread. He wasn't hungry for food; he hungered for God. He knew departure was near, by death or by the return of Jesus.

*This might be the crowning day.* John staggered to the mouth of the cave to gaze at the eastern sky, but not too close so that his parishioners could see him. He remained in the shadows, looking east...praying...hoping.

*Maybe today...* He closed his eyes and again prayed, "Even so come, Lord Jesus...."

A rooster crowed in the distance as John listened to the waves breaking over the rocky coast. On winter days such as this one, the entire sky was overcast and fog covered the island. Yet, even though the day—cold as death—chilled his bones and the sun remained hidden, John knew it was still there, just as knew God was near even though He couldn't be touched.

The brisk morning breeze promised a storm, but John didn't mind angry weather; he anticipated God doing something special today. Dragging his frail body back into the cave, he again bypassed the bread and water and knelt at his usual spot.

Because John's faith expected God to do something special today, the Lord responded. The Spirit of God filled the room—it was the atmospheric presence of God, and John could feel Him, just as he had earlier felt the cold misty breeze whipping through his hair. Was he experiencing another Pentecost, when the Spirit of God had fallen on the disciples in the upper room?

"Are You coming back today?" John asked in prayer. "Why not come back today to deliver Your Church?"

John didn't pray for himself. He didn't mind imprisonment—he had no family left. John didn't have any future hope of more evangelism—he was too old to travel. John didn't have any place he needed to visit—he had seen all he wanted to see. John had come to the end of the road, and it ended on this forsaken island. With no more dreams, an old man could do nothing else than pray...

"Lord Jesus, I worship You...Lord Jesus, I thank You...Lord Jesus, come...."

## Your Time to Worship

Thank You, God, that I'm alive, that I can wake up, and that I have another opportunity to praise You.

Thank You, God, that my problems are not greater than they are, that my health is not as bad as it could be, and that I have a desire to worship You.

Lord, I expect You to return any moment. Forgive me for not being ready and for putting off Your tasks, while filling my life with selfish things.

Lord, thank You for the excitement I get thinking You might return today, that my problems will be over, that my imprisoned body will be free, that I can touch You in worship, and that You will touch me.

Lord, You are great in power to bring me to this place in life. You are loving in generosity to overlook my past mistakes. You are patient with me, even when I forget Your tasks.

Lord, I praise You for this moment in time, for the opportunity of today, and that I can worship You now!

Believers on Patmos had no comforts and little food; they were separated from their families and homes. Rome was persecuting believers for their allegiance to another King—throwing them to lions, burning them at the stake, beating them, torturing them, simply because their supreme allegiance was to Jesus Christ.

Again, tears came from his closed eyes…

"Come quickly, Lord Jesus."

With that prayer, John felt an inner urge, almost an inner compulsion. It was the same inner drive he had felt when he wrote the Gospel, the one they call "The Gospel of John." John quickly obeyed, as quickly as a man over 90 years can react. Approaching the table, he pushed aside the bread and cup. Taking papyrus paper the other prisoners had made for him from the reeds found in the small inlet between LaScala and Merika, he dipped a feather quill into ink,

"I will write what the Spirit tells me."

"Write what's on your heart," the Spirit told John.

His first morning thought was…Jesus. His last thought before sleep was…Jesus. More than anything else, John wanted to be with Jesus. John remembered what the Master had promised the night before He died…

"I will come again and receive you to Myself." John wept again at the memory of that Last Supper before He died, because Jesus assured him, "Where I am, there you will be with Me."

"That's it," John spoke out loud, but no one was there to hear him. "I know what I will write. I will write a book about the return of Jesus Christ. I will encourage believers everywhere because the Savior is coming back for them." Then he spoke the words in a dark room.

"Jesus is coming…"

How would he begin? What would be the first word of this final book? John thought about the Apocalypse…about believers going to Heaven…about unbelievers thrown into hell…about tribulations…about vision. But John didn't want to write just the black parts of the coming judgment. He continued to look within his heart for the things to write. John didn't find hatred in his heart for Rome; he didn't pray for wrath on his persecutors. The only desire of his heart was Jesus. The only object of his love was Jesus Christ. He scratched the first phrase on paper…

"The Revelation of Jesus Christ…"

He would write about the coming of Jesus. He repeated the phrase softly.

"The Revelation of Jesus Christ."

John was pleased with his first words—they represented the passion of his life…Jesus Christ. He had written a gospel account of the past life of Jesus; now he would write of Jesus' coming in the future. This book would focus the reader on Jesus—not on judgment, not on tribulation, not on miraculous signs in the sky when stars would fall and battles would be fought all over the world.

John carefully penned the words, "From Jesus Who is…From Jesus Who was…and From Jesus Who is to come."

Again, dipping his feather quill into the black ink that the prisoners had made from soot and olive oil, John wrote, "From Jesus our faithful witness…from Jesus, the First Begotten from the dead…from Jesus, the Prince of all kings on earth."

The Spirit of God came upon John as he wrote the book. He was borne along as his pen etched words on paper. At times, the bony fingers wrote what he knew from the depth of his heart. Then at other times, John wrote about things he didn't know. As the Spirit of God whispered in his ear, John wrote the message on paper.

"Unto Jesus who loved us and washed us from our sins in His own blood."

Every time John wrote the name *Jesus*, he would stop and put down his quill to praise his Master. "Thank You, Jesus!" The aged apostle talked to Jesus, even though His Master was not physically present in the cave. It was the way he had prayed for years. The aged ears of John could still hear Jesus talk to him. Though there were no sounds in the room, John knew what Jesus was saying to him, just as he had heard Jesus whisper to him at the Last Supper when he leaned on the Master's breast. John was fellowshipping with Jesus—communing with Jesus—and John knew he couldn't leave the presence of Jesus. There would be no sermon today; he'd be fellowshipping with Jesus all day...he'd be writing all day...all week...all month, for he was to write a lengthy book. He was writing the Book of Revelation—the last Book of the Bible.

## Your Time to Worship

Jesus, thank You for being my *forgiver* of sins, my *reconciler* to God, my *resurrection* from the dead, and my *eternal life*.

Jesus, I worship You for being the *Creator* of all things past, the *Baby* of Bethlehem, and the *Returning Judge* of sin.

Jesus, I praise You for Your constant *love*, Your *purity*, and Your restraining *patience*.

Jesus, give me *wisdom* to know what to do today. Be my *strength* to overcome problems, and my *guide* to always do right.

Even though John didn't come out of the cave, his small church of prisoners continued to wait...watch...pray. Though raggedly dressed and malnourished, their greatest desire was for John to get a message from God for them. Patiently, they prayed as John wrote...

"Jesus the Alpha and Omega...Jesus the Almighty...Jesus the Beginning and the End...Jesus Who is...Jesus Who was...Jesus Who is to come."

The prisoners waited a long time for John that day as he began a writing project we now call the Book of Revelation. It's the last Book of the Bible, and John thought it was probably the last work he would write before he died or before Jesus returned to earth.

What did John do when He faced the end? He did the same thing you should do. Whether you are coming to the end of physical life or to the conclusion of your failed dreams—a place where you can do nothing else—you should worship.

### What I Learned From John's Worship

I can worship Jesus when I approach death.

I can worship Jesus when I am a prisoner to my circumstances.

I can continually draw closer to Jesus even though I've walked with Him all my life.

My memory is an excellent help to intimate worship.

I can meet Jesus in worship, even though I'm waiting for His physical return.

## Section One

### Scripture: Revelation 1:1-20

Lord, I want a revelation from You—speak to me;
       Teach me truth—where You've been;
       Show me revelation—who You are!
   Unveil to me the future judgment on this earth,
       The events surrounding Your rapture and return.
       But most of all, unveil Jesus to me.
   Just as You sent an angel to reveal to John
       The things that are to come in the future,
       Reveal them to me.
   John wrote down everything he heard and saw.
       Now, may I read it and learn.
   Lord, bless me as I read Your revelation,
       And enrich my life with what I learn,
       Because the time of Your return is close.

Lord, John wrote to seven churches in Asia Minor,
       Praying peace and grace for them
       From Jesus Who is, Who was, and Who is coming.

Jesus, I worship You the faithful witness,
       The firstborn from the dead,
       The Ruler of the kings of the earth.

Jesus, I thank You for loving me,
       For freeing me from sin by Your blood,
       And giving me the intercessory role of a priest
       Forever and ever, Amen.

Lord Jesus is coming with clouds,
>Just as He left the earth with clouds.
>I will see Him, along with every other person;
>>Even those who crucified Him will see Him.
>And they along with every other person who rejected Him
>Will mourn because they are not ready to meet Him.

Lord, I worship Jesus, my Alpha and Omega.
>>He is the Lord God Almighty.
>>He was, He is, and He is coming.

Lord, John suffered because of His faith;
>>He was patiently Kingdom-bound.
>John was imprisoned on Patmos Island
>>Because he preached Jesus and witnessed to lost people.

On a Sunday the Holy Spirit filled him,
>>And he heard a voice behind him
>>That awakened him like a trumpet.
>The voice was Jesus' who told John,
>>"Write down everything I show you
>And send it to seven churches:
>>Ephesus, Smyrna, Pergamos, Thyatira, Sardis,
>>Philadelphia, and Laodicea."
>Then John turned to see the Person speaking to him.
>>He saw seven golden candlesticks in a circle;
>>Jesus—the Son of Man—was standing in the middle.
>Jesus had on a long robe tied with a golden band (sash).
>>John could barely make out His head;
>His hair was shining brilliantly,
>>Like the sun reflecting off white snow.
>The eyes of Jesus were aflame with anger,
>>Burning through the lies and sins of sinners.
>His feet gleamed like polished bronze,
>>And His voice thundered away every other sound,

Like mighty waves breaking on a rocky shore.
Jesus had seven stars in His right hand.
The words of His mouth cut like the sharpest sword.
His face glistened like the blinding sun.

Lord, John fell at His feet like one dropping dead;
I too fall to worship at His feet.
"Do not be afraid," Jesus tells us,
"For there is no fear to those who worship Me."
Jesus said, "I am the First and the Last,
I am the Living One who lives eternally."
Jesus continued, "I was dead but now I am alive;
I will live forever and ever;
I have the keys to death and hell."

Lord, when I face the threats of dying or judgment,
I will listen for the jingle of the keys,
For I know You're coming to deliver me.

Lord, You told John to write all he saw presently happening,
And what You showed him that was coming.
The seven stars in the hand of Christ
Were the seven pastors of the seven churches.
And the seven golden candlesticks
Were the seven churches to which He is writing.
Amen.

# Section Two

# WORSHIP:
# WAITING IN JESUS' PRESENCE
# FOR HIS MESSAGE

### Scripture: Revelation 2:1–3:22

The cave's thick blackness was held back by the tiny flame flickering in the olive oil lamp. The prisoners had insisted that John the apostle always have the lamp lit when he was awake; they wanted him to be able to write down anything the Spirit of God spoke. John carefully squeezed his quill, sucking ink into its tiny cylinder, and then he barely squeezed the feather, squirting a tiny flow of ink from the point of the feather onto the paper. The wet black ink formed words—wonderful words of life—from the mind of John and the heart of the Holy Spirit. He wrote…

"I am Jesus Who walks among the churches to determine their faithfulness and I hold their pastors in my hand. Write letters to the leaders of the seven churches to warn them of the coming tribulation that Christians will face."

John reread the words he had just written, then blew on the paper to dry the ink. He thought, *Will I die in this tribulation…or will Jesus return to transform this frail body into a glorified body like His?* It mattered not to John if he died, for that would be better—he would be with Christ.

John had difficulty keeping his mind focused on writing. When he thought about Jesus walking among the churches, he thought about the spiritual condition of each church. Some were spiritually energetic; but in contrast, some were carnal and dabbling in sin.

All old men often have trouble with their memory, their attention span, and their mental focus. John was old, so his thoughts drifted...but his thoughts drifted to Jesus.

A friend once asked John why he could remember the details of his life for the three and a half years he had spent with Jesus before the cross, but couldn't remember where he left his tunic a few moments ago. John answered, "Jesus is as real to me now as He was back then." He continued, "When I'm sitting on the rocks watching the sea waves, Jesus is with me...I talk to Him...I listen to Him." John explained that it was easy to keep focused when talking to a real person—"Jesus is with me everywhere I go. I see Him with the eyes of my heart, although I can't see Him with my physical eyes."

The flame in the candle on the table almost flickered out. The fingers of darkness leaped momentarily into the cave until the tiny fire in the light caught new life.

"Ansel!" John called to the young prisoner who waited on him. "More oil."

The diligent servant did not want to disturb John's thoughts or break his concentration. He rushed into the cave without speaking...without eye contact...and tried to be as inconspicuous as possible, while quickly replenishing the lamp on the table.

"Can I get you anything else?" Ansel reluctantly asked the question, not wanting to interrupt the old man's communion with the Lord. The other prisoners expected him to take care of John's every need.

"Nothing," John answered. Then he smiled. "I need nothing except new eyes and a steady hand." John knew he had much writing to do. Ansel returned the smile, then assured the apostle of his prayers.

"The prisoners are outside on their knees praying for you," Ansel remarked. "They are praying for the Holy Spirit to give you a message for them today."

"Go tell them to pray harder," John told his associate. "Jesus is giving me a message for them—and all the churches. Pray vigorously. Jesus has a message for all Christians."

Ansel left, and John turned again to his writing. He looked at the half-filled sheet of paper but could not determine what to write next. At first, he had written frivolously, but now his mind was blank. Was this writer's block? An old man's memory lapse? Or had the Spirit stopped speaking to him?

*I'll pray,* John thought. *I'll let God guide me regarding what to write.* He then knelt beside the table, his bony knees scraping against the rock hard floor that they had grown accustomed to.

Praying, John asked the Lord what to write. Although he didn't receive an immediate answer, a picture came to his mind—it was Jesus. All he could think of was Jesus. The Lord didn't tell John what to write; instead, the Lord's presence entered the room. John felt it, just as a person can tell when someone enters a room behind him. No longer could he remain kneeling. He dropped from his knees to bow prostrate with his face to the ground—the only way to worship.

John had experienced the atmospheric presence of God many times before, but this time he felt different.

## Your Time to Worship

Lord, I know You are everywhere present in Your omnipresence.

Lord, I know You are around me and indwelling me.

Lord, I want Your atmospheric presence here now as I worship You.

Lord, I thank You for dying to forgive my sins, and rising from the dead to give me new life.

Lord, I am grateful for my conversion from my old life and for the new desires You create within me.

Lord, I thank You for all I've received in salvation, making me a new creature in Christ.

> Lord, I worship You because You are everything I need, and I want to please You in everything I do.

Then hearing something, the ancient apostle's memory was pricked. *Are my ears playing tricks on me?* he thought. What John thought he was hearing made his heart jump; his eyes blinked, and he turned his best ear toward the sound. He had to be sure. It was a voice he had heard 60 years earlier, and it was a voice he could never forget.

The voice was not just a memory, nor was he dreaming, nor was it a vision. The voice was actually speaking. His ears were hearing an audible voice! And it was not the voice of his assistant, nor the voice of any one of the Christian prisoners, nor of a Roman guard.

Slowly, John arose, first to one knee; then he pushed up on the chair to rise to his feet. He heard the voice echoing off the granite walls of the cave from the shadows behind him; but the apostle didn't need to call out, "Who is it?" nor did he need to turn to see who it was who had spoken to him. He knew.

John recognized the voice—one that he could never forget. It was the same voice that first called to him, and now, Jesus was audibly commanding him what to write:

"I walk among the churches to determine their faithfulness. These seven will represent all churches that are scattered around the Mediterranean world, and they will represent future churches scattered throughout time—till I come. These seven letters will represent the strengths of some churches, but also, I will tell you of the complacency and sins of other churches. Write so that all churches will know how to prepare for the coming tribulation and My second return to earth."

Even before Jesus told John what seven churches to include, John's mind began to wander and consider various churches he knew. He first thought of the church in Ephesus, the church he had been pastoring when arrested. The Ephesian church was a good church, but with time they had lost some of their fire for evangelism.

This church, in turn, had planted many other churches surrounding Ephesus. Some were great missionary churches, such as Philadelphia. However, another one had been infected with sexual sins and idolatry—Thyatira. Then there was the lazy church—Laodicea...

Deciding to put a hold on his roaming thoughts, John determined, *I will wait for Jesus to tell me what churches to include in my manuscripts.*

In the meantime, the fading light of the small candle was overwhelmed by the magnificent light of Jesus Christ. His light glistened off the walls of the cave as His presence filled the room. John was no longer experiencing the cave, as God's blazing glory had now transformed it into a sanctuary. His heart soared as he entered the presence of God.

It was no longer another Sunday to worship the Lord. Today was truly the Lord's Day, for the Lord had come to John. Jesus was here!

## What I Learned About Prayer From This Account of John Seeing Jesus

I can pray to meet Jesus even when I think I'm far from Him, even when stuck in the "caves" of this life.

I don't think of food or other physical comforts when I meet Jesus.

I will worship Jesus better when I remember what He has done for me.

I have difficulty describing Jesus because of His divine perfection and my human limitation.

I respond in speechless admiration when I'm in His presence.

I am touched by Jesus for a task when He comes to me.

## Section Two

## Scripture: Revelation 2:1–3:22

*To Ephesus: The Good Church (2:2-7)*

Lord, John wrote to the leaders of the church at Ephesus,
>"This is the message of the One holding the seven stars,
>Who is walking in the middle of the churches."
Jesus knows everything that the Ephesian Christians do,
>Realizing their hard work and patience in trials.
Jesus knows they don't tolerate sin among their members,
>And they test imposters claiming to be preachers,
>Revealing their false teaching.
Jesus knows they have patiently suffered for Him,
>Without giving up and quitting.
Jesus has some complaints about the Ephesians—
>They have lost their first love for Him.

Lord, when I lose my first love for You,
>I will remember those times when I was first saved
>And go back to doing what I originally did.

Lord, Jesus said He will come and remove their testimony
>If they do not repent;
>Their candlestick will no longer stand with other churches.

But Jesus notes some good things about them—
>They hate the deeds of the lustful Nicolaitans,
>Because God hates fleshly sin.
Jesus warns them, "Those who have ears
>To hear spiritual messages,
>Listen to what the Holy Spirit is saying to the churches.

Those who live victorious over sin,
        Will eat from the tree of life in Paradise."

## To Smyrna: The Persecuted Church (2:8-11)

Lord, John wrote to the leader of the church at Smyrna,
        "This is the message from the First, and Last,
        The One who died and came back to life."
Jesus knows all their trials and sufferings,
        And He knows their poverty, while they are rich
        In heavenly treasures.
Jesus knows the slanderous accusations against them
        By religious people who claim to know God,
        Whose house of worship is satan's home.
Jesus says, "Don't be afraid of coming sufferings.
        Some of you will be tested by imprisonment;
        You will be persecuted for a time.
Even if you have to die for Me—be faithful;
        You will receive the crown of life.
If you have ears to hear spiritual messages,
        Listen to what the Holy Spirit is saying to the churches.
Those who are victorious
        Have nothing to fear in the second death."

## To Pergamum: The Tolerant Church (2:12-17)

Lord, John wrote to the church leader at Pergamum,
        From Jesus who has the sharp sword
        To divide between error and truth.
Jesus knows where you live is the place
        Where satan rules and controls.
Jesus knows they are holding firmly to His name
        And do not deny Him when persecuted.
Jesus knows Antipas who was a faithful witness,

Who was martyred before their eyes
By the followers of satan.

But Jesus has some complaints against them;
Some "Christians" have been following Balaam,
Who taught Balak to compromise.
So, Israel commits adultery and sacrifices to idols.
Jesus also knows that some "Christians" have accepted
The teachings of the Nicolaitans.
Jesus tells them, "Repent, or I will come to
Judge you with the truth of the Word of God.
If you have ears to hear spiritual messages,
Listen to what the Holy Spirit is saying to the churches.
Those who are victorious will receive
Hidden manna from Heaven to strengthen them,
And their new names will be engraved on a white stone.
And no one knows what it is, but those who receive it."

## To Thyatira: The Compromising Church (2:18-29)

Lord, John wrote to the leader of the church of Thyatira,
"This is the message of the Son of God,
Who has eyes penetrating like a flaming fire,
Whose feet will judge all sin."
Jesus knows all about them—their good works,
And their love, faith, and patience,
And that they are still growing in grace.

But Jesus has a complaint against them—
They permit a woman like Jezebel
To teach and prophesy among them.
She entices Christians away from the true faith
By getting them to commit adultery
And sacrifice to an idol and eat its food.
Jesus tells her to repent and change her ways,

But she has not given up her adulterous ways.
Jesus will bring suffering to her life,
    And those who commit adultery with her
    Will suffer intently unless they repent.
Her children will die prematurely under judgment,
    So all churches will realize that
Jesus continually searches deeply into hearts
    To give people what their behavior deserves.

Jesus does not condemn faithful Christians in Thyatira
    Who have not followed the teachings of Jezebel,
    Nor learned the "deep secrets" of satan.
Jesus tells the faithful ones to hold firmly to their faith
    Until the second coming.
Those who are victorious
    And continue serving until the end
    Will receive power over the nations.
They will rule by absolute authority like a rod of iron
    In the millennium with Jesus Christ,
And crush all rebellion against righteousness.
    Then Jesus will reward them with the morning star.
"If you have ears to hear spiritual messages,
    Listen to what the Holy Spirit is saying to the churches."

## To Sardis: The Sleeping Church (3:1-6)

Lord, John wrote to the leader of the church at Sardis,
    "This is the message from the One holding
    The seven spirits of God and the seven stars."
Jesus knows their reputation as an alive church,
    Yet they are inwardly dead.
"Wake up, revive what little you have left
    Because you are about to die."
Jesus has not seen anything in them
    That is commendable to God.

He tells them to remember what they hear,
And to hold on to the Gospel.
He tells them to repent and wake up,
Otherwise, He will come unexpectedly to judge them
Like a thief in the night.

Jesus says there are a few Christians in Sardis
Who haven't dirtied their clothes with evil.
They are fit to walk with Him
Because they are clothed in spotless garments.
Those who are victorious will be dressed in white.
Their names will not be blotted from the Book of Life,
And Jesus will acknowledge them to the Father.
"If you have ears to hear spiritual messages,
Listen to what the Holy Spirit is saying to the churches."

*To Philadelphia: The Church of the Open Door (3:7-13)*

Lord, John wrote to the leader of the church of Philadelphia,
"This is a message from Jesus, the Holy and Faithful One,
Who has the keys of David,
From the One who can open what no one can shut,
And shut what no one can open."

Jesus knows all about the Philadelphians.
They have an open door of opportunity
That no one is able to shut.
Jesus knows they are not a strong church,
Yet they have kept His commandments,
And have not denied His name.
Jesus will judge those in the false church,
Who wrongly claim to be Christians,
Making them bow at His feet at the Great White
Judgment Throne,
And they will acknowledge that the Philadelphia Church

was right.
Jesus will protect the Philadelphian Christians
     In the hour of the Great Tribulation,
Which will come upon the whole world,
     Testing believers to determine their faithfulness.
Jesus wants them to hold firmly to their faith,
     And not let anyone take away their rewards,
     Because He will be with them.
Jesus will make those who are victorious over sin
     Like a pillar in the Temple of God,
     And they will be tested no more.
Jesus will write God's name on them,
     And they will be inhabitants of the New Jerusalem,
     The city that will come down from God in Heaven.
"If you have ears to hear spiritual messages,
     Listen to what the Holy Spirit is saying to the churches."

*To Laodicea: The Self-satisfied Church (3:14-22)*

Lord, John wrote to the leader of the church at Laodicea,
     "This is the message of Jesus, the faithful
     and true Witness,
     The One who created worlds."
Jesus knows that they are not hot or cold;
     He wants them to be one or the other.
But because the Christians at Laodicea are lukewarm,
     He will spit them out of His mouth.
The Laodiceans are claiming to be rich,
     That they have everything they need;
But they don't realize they are wretched,
     Miserably poor, blind, and naked.
Jesus warns them to buy from Him,
     Gold purified by fire,
     That will make them truly rich.

Jesus tells them to dress themselves in righteousness,
> Like pure white robes to cover their spiritual nakedness.

Put spiritual ointment on their blinded eyes,
> So they can have spiritual insight.

Jesus says, "I am the One who rebukes and disciplines
> All of My followers whom I love."

Therefore, repent from your indifferences,
> And take a stand for righteousness and diligence.

Jesus says, "I am standing at the door of this opportunity,
> Knocking to see if you will open to Me.

If you hear My voice and open the door,
> I will come in to spiritually feed you."

Those who are victorious will share the throne of Jesus
> Just as He was victorious over death,
> And took His place at the right hand of the Father.

"If you have ears to hear spiritual messages,
> Listen to what the Holy Spirit is saying to the churches."
> Amen.

# Section Three

# WORSHIP:
## IMMEDIATELY UPON ENTERING HEAVEN

### Scripture: Revelation 4:1-11

The heavy rain cloud passed over Patmos that Sunday morning, taking the threat of a storm away. Toward the middle of the day, the early morning fog evaporated under the warming sun. Like a warm inviting ray of light peering through a crack in a heavy timber door, a few golden beams of sunlight intermittently shown between the slits in the clouds to fall on the backs of the prisoners praying in front of the cave. The warm sun encouraged them to continue praying for John.

But inside the cave, John couldn't see the sunlight, nor could he feel its gentle warmth. He had lost all sense of time, busily writing his book of future events. Each time he finished a sentence he paused to pray, asking God to direct the next phrase...the next idea...the next page. It was not his book he was writing; it was God's book...God's Word...The Revelation of Jesus Christ. He prayed...

"Lord, thank You for speaking to me...thank You for using me to write Your message...thank You for loving me..."

The apostle John was known for his oft repeated phrases, such as, "God is love." Back in Ephesus—at the church he loved—when John sat on the pulpit too feeble to preach a sermon, he'd simply exhort the congregation...

"Children, love one another, because God is love."

That was a sermon in itself.

John wanted to be near the heart of God. He wanted to know God…feel God…touch God…experience God. When a person wants to get as close as possible to God, the Lord reacts in kind, and God reveals Himself to him.

When Enoch walked close to God, there came a day when God took Enoch from this earth to live with Him in Heaven. No one else has since received that privilege. When Moses grew close to God, his face shone. Likewise, Stephen's face glowed when he repudiated the wicked demands of the Sanhedrin. Then they stoned him to death.

John wanted to know God intimately. Would God snatch up John to Heaven as He had Enoch? No!

Would John's face shine as Moses' had? Or would his face glow as Stephen's did when he was stoned? No!

God had another plan for old John. He would do something no other could do. Jesus was revealing Himself to the apostle so that he could write a book about the future. John would see the future; and from henceforth, John would be called the Seer. He would write a book of the revelation of the future, and he would be called John, the Revelator.

In that gruesome cave of black stone and cold damp walls, John would soon see the glorious city of light and bask in the warm light of Heaven. Only ten brisk steps from one wall of the cave to the other, but from that cramped little prison, John would be transposed into eternity to God's dwelling place that has no walls…no limits…no yesterdays…no tomorrows.

Was John's Spirit transported to experience future events while his body remained confined to the small cave? Or was John's whole body taken there? What do you think?

Perhaps John only had "eternity eyes" to see the future as God showed him one vision after another. Or, did he leave the cave? Did he vicariously experience the future from the isle prison? When you get to Heaven, ask God to tell you what really happened to John on Patmos. For now, you the reader can determine for yourself.

Meanwhile, in the cave, John prayed, "I worship You, Lord...I'll do what You tell me to do...I'll be what You want me to be...I'll write what You want me to write."

## Your Time to Worship

Lord, show me what You want me to do for You while I wait for Your return. Holy Spirit, lead me!

Lord, I'll do what You want me to do. Holy Spirit, empower me!

Lord, I often fail You, and I'm often too weak to serve You properly. Holy Spirit, help me!

Lord, I want to improve on the things I do for You. Holy Spirit, teach me!

Lord, help me not procrastinate with my responsibilities, because You are coming back soon. Holy Spirit, quicken me!

Lord, because I know You are coming for me, and will receive me to Yourself, I worship You in anticipation. Holy Spirit, receive me.

The Lord knew John would be a trusty instrument. Just as he picked up his quill to write on paper, God picked up John in His divine hand to write the holy Word of God. God would write a book through John, and He said...

"Write the things I will show you...things of the past...things of the present...things of the future."

Bowing, the old apostle nodded his head in obedience and whispered, "I will write what You show me."

When John submitted, the Lord showed him a door…it was the door to Heaven. From deep in the bowels of Mount Elias, John looked up through the ceiling of the cave…past the sun and stars…past the future; John looked into Heaven through a door.

When John blinked his eyes, he didn't lose sight of the door. Even with his eyes shut, he could still see the door. He couldn't get the door out of his sight. John looked into the heart of God through the door into Heaven…the door…the hinges…the latch…all as real as though he stood at the actual entrance to Heaven itself. Then a loud authoritative voice invited him to enter,

"COME UP HITHER!"

The voice told John he would go through that door to enter Heaven and see the future. He would then write the events that he saw in Heaven in a book. The voice explained…

"I WILL SHOW YOU THINGS THAT WILL HAPPEN HEREAFTER."

When the door to Heaven opened, John entered. He remembered 60 years ago hearing Jesus say, "I Am the Door…" All who enter Heaven are followers of Jesus. Those who believe in Jesus enter Heaven through Jesus, the Door.

Immediately, John was whisked away in the Spirit from Patmos through the door into Heaven itself. John's spirit left the cave on Patmos, soaring through the few remaining black clouds over the Aegean Sea, past the flaming sun, past trillions of stars, through Heaven's door, to enter the presence of God.

The first thing John saw was God's throne—its brilliance was like the sun itself, and John could look at nothing else. The penetrating light was so blinding that John was not able to see the One sitting on the throne. Then he remembered the Scriptures…

"No man can see God." The old apostle realized that even in Heaven he couldn't look upon God, for an infinite God is "unseeable" with mere human eyes.

Nothing else commanded John's attention. He did not ask to see Zebedee his father or his mother. He didn't think of Mary, the mother of Jesus—the one whose care was given to him by Jesus from the cross. No thought of Abraham, Moses, or David. John couldn't take his eyes off the throne of God, nor could he think of anything else but the captivating vision of God at the center of Heaven.

Beautiful colors flashed intermittently from the throne—the green sparkle of an emerald, the red glow of a ruby, the blue hue of a sapphire, and the captivating and glistening white of a diamond.

John stood transfixed, staring at the throne of God...afraid to move...afraid to think...afraid the scene would go away. He drank deeply of all he saw, because he wanted to remember what he saw.

Finally, John, still in awe at the sight of God's throne, slowly began to gaze upon other magnificent sights in Heaven. The next objects to attract his attention were 24 smaller thrones surrounding the throne of God. Each throne faced God, and each occupant worshiped Him.

Again, John's response was to drop to his knees to worship God. He remembered that he had been told to write what he saw. Although his memory was not as clear now as it had been when he was a youth, he knew that if he would be obedient to Jesus...if he would give diligence to see, then the Spirit would help him remember when it came time to write. The promise of Jesus at the Last Supper came back to John...

"The Holy Spirit will bring all things to your remembrance."

John carefully counted the 24 thrones. Were these 12 thrones for the Old Testament saints? Were they for the 12 sons of Jacob? He didn't know. Were they for 12 judges...12 prophets...12 chosen leaders? Or did the 12 Old Testament thrones stand for all believers before the cross—12 representing the Jewish number of completion?

John wondered about the remaining 12 thrones. Who were these thrones for? Were they for 12 New Testament leaders? During His earthly life,

Jesus had promised the 12 disciples they would sit on 12 thrones in the Kingdom. Would He sit on one of these thrones? Would Paul be sitting on the 12th, the one abdicated by Judas Iscariot? Or would these 12 thrones be symbolic of believers *after* the cross?

As John turned his eyes away from God's throne, he began to survey Heaven itself. In front of the throne was a large sea, a calm sea without a ripple upon the face of the water. This silent sea in Heaven reminded John of his youth when the early morning Sea of Galilee was like glass as the wind held back its breath. Once, John rowed out early before sunrise upon the motionless water. Each dip of his oar into the still water created a concentric circle of waves; his boat left the only wake on the sea. John remembered that rowing on that lake was one of the most peaceful experiences of his life. It was there on the Sea of Galilee that John as a young man worshiped God. Now, the sea before the throne of God filled his thoughts of peace—perfect peace. Here, John as an old man worshiped God.

At the four corners of God's throne were angels—four Seraphims. Among their other duties, the angelic sentries guarded the throne. Not that God needed guarding, or that anyone could guard God. Nevertheless, they were positioned at the four corners of God's throne, not so much to protect God, but for the protection of the inhabitants of Heaven. Just as on earth no one could approach God, so in Heaven, the glory of God kept all creatures at their distance. Even when God appeared on Mount Sinai to give the Ten Commandment to Moses, the people were warned not to come near the mountain, or even touch it, lest they die.

The Seraphim who stood near God knew certain things about the past, the present, and the future to come. They knew all they needed to know as though they had eyes on every side of their head.

As protectors of God, the Seraphim were enormously powerful, yet only God is omnipotent—only God has all power. The Seraphim were imminently intelligent, yet only God is omniscient—God knows everything past, present, and the future, and everything that might happen, but will not happen. The Seraphim could travel everywhere, yet only God is omnipresent—only God is everywhere present at the same time.

The Seraphim were more than protectors; they were also given the task of singing worship songs and were the worship leaders of Heaven. When they praised God, all people followed their lead. All the time—without stopping—the Seraphim sang praises...

"Holy...Holy...Holy...Lord God Almighty."

Constantly throughout Heaven, the continuous voices of the four Seraphim could be heard praising God. They sang a threefold exaltation:

"Holy to the Father...

Holy to the Son...

Holy to the Spirit..."

John had seen more than he could assimilate; his knowledge exceeded his experience. He could wait no longer and again dropped to his knees and lifted his hands in worship with the angels to the Triune Deity.

"Holy...Holy...Holy...!"

The creaking voice of the ancient disciple echoed off the walls of that cave in Patmos. John was singing, from the bottom of his heart, the threefold Amen with the Seraphim. Any human ears that heard John that day would not have understood his heart for they could hear only his voice. They could hear only the exuberant voice of an old man praising God. But if they could have seen his face, they would have known his deep satisfaction. And if they were filled with the Spirit, they too would have worshiped with John, for John was worshiping in the Spirit.

While John worshiped, he heard the Seraphim sing additional words of praise, and John joined them, "Lord God Almighty, who was in the past...who is now reigning...who will reign forever in the future."

## Your Time to Worship

Lord, Your holiness is a glaring contrast to my unrighteousness and uncleanness. Forgive me; don't look on my sins!

Lord, Your holiness makes You infinitely superior to anything I am or I do. Forgive my sin and give me a desire to be holy!

Lord, You stand above and beyond me in holiness, higher than any existence I know or experience. Forgive my failures and lift me to You!

Lord, Your infinite greatness and power make me realize how small and weak I am. Forgive my weaknesses and give me strength!

Lord, Your holy standards are so pure I cannot attain them. Forgive me and make me perfect in Christ!

Lord, You have remained holy and majestic, no matter how much I resist and oppose You. Forgive my doubts and give me a heart to worship You!

As a boy, John had gone to the synagogue in Capernaum where he heard his neighbors sing the Psalms of David. Eventually, the young lad worshiped God with the words of David as he sang them in the congregation with other sinners like himself. He, like they, sought salvation from God. This worship of redeemed sinners had been wonderful in its gratitude; but angelic worship, the worship of the Seraphim in Heaven, was different. The four angels had never sinned, so they had not experienced God's reconciliation.

As a boy, John's singing in the synagogue was different from the four Seraphim who worshiped out of a pure Spirit that never disobeyed God.

John knew he had sinned, while the Seraphim knew they had never once disobeyed. The Seraphim were singing—not better than the redeemed families of Capernaum—and not worse. The angels' perfect voices do not make them perfect, even though they worship with perfect music. Rather, the sincerity of their spirit makes their worship perfect.

Likewise, John's imperfect songs, sung with a scratchy voice in off-pitch harmony along with the Capernaum congregation, did not make his worship less than Heaven's worship. The perfection of worship is judged by its object, not by the human who gives praise. Both the angels and the people of Capernaum focused their worship on God. The extent of worship is judged by its sincerity. Both the angels who never sinned, and the forgiven fishermen of Capernaum who knew they were sinners, poured worship out of unfettered vessels. Perfect worship comes from perfect sincerity.

John sang with the four angels—his raspy voice joining their pristine music—to worship God who always has been…who now reigns…and who will always exist.

The four angels sang loudly, "GLORY TO GOD…FOR GOD IS GREAT!"

John repeated their words, adding "Amen."

The four angels sang loudly again, "HONOR…LET GOD BE EXALTED."

John repeated their words again adding, "Amen."

The four angels repeated loudly a third shout, "THANKS TO GOD FOR ALL HE'S DONE."

John wept for he was grateful for all that God had done for him. He remembered being a hotheaded selfish disciple who had arrogantly asked Jesus to call fire down from Heaven to destroy the Samaritans who had rejected the Master. He prayed…

"Thank You for being patient with me and forgiving me."

John remembered selfishly begging Jesus to appoint him over the other 12 disciples. Now in Heaven he worshiped…

"Thank You for letting me be Your slave."

Many times in Jerusalem, John had heard the best Levitical musicians in all Israel sing in the temple to the glory of God. But even the Levitical singers in Jerusalem had never inspired the awe he was experiencing now. His Spirit was lifted with their voices as they worshiped…

"GLORY TO HIM WHO SITS ON THE THRONE…"

"I agree," John whispered from his cold cave.

"HONOR TO HIM WHO SITS ON THE THRONE…"

"Amen," John again agreed with the worship voices.

"THANKS TO HIM WHO SITS ON THE THRONE."

With silent tears, John offered his human understanding of thanksgiving along with the perfect understanding of those in Heaven. Then the 24 saints arose out of their thrones as one man. They looked not at one another, nor did they wait for a signal. Each responded according to the personal hunger of their heart. Each acting independently, yet with homogeneous unity, they all together fell on their faces to worship God, each praising Him with his total being.

Then each saint took the crown from upon his head, the crown given to them by God as recognition of their faithfulness on earth. Each of them now realized they were not worthy of the reward. If each had exhibited any kind of faithfulness, it was because of God's grace to them. With open hands, the crowns were held out to God.

John recognized their gestures. When a poor landowner appealed to King Caesar, he usually brought a gift—an animal, an offering of food, a sack of gold coins. This gift was designed by the pleading landowner to appease Caesar. When the gift was offered with outstretched hands, Caesar either took it or rejected it according to the pangs of his conscience or the reasonable judgment of his mind.

The crown had been given to each of the 24 saints because of what each had done on earth. The crowns represented their best achievements. When each arrived in Heaven, they were met by God who embraced them, "Well done, thou good and faithful servant." Then God gave them a crown of reward. Each crown represented a different kind of glory that was brought to God. Some received a crown of life for soul-winning. Some didn't have great opportunities for evangelism, but were faithful when persecuted, receiving a crown of life. Some, who in spite of hardships, faithfully watched for the return of Jesus and received a crown of righteousness.

The 24 saints offered their crowns to God. Their crowns were more precious than money, position, fame, or fine clothes. Yet, each elder realized without the grace of God, they would have had no opportunity to serve God or bring glory to God. It was the strength of God in them who gave them any ability to work for Him. Thus, each elder offered his crown back to God in Heaven, just as they had offered everything to God on earth.

John curiously watched the ceremony. He watched to see if God would take the crowns from them. He remembered an occasion when Caesar had given a gift back to the landowner. It was Caesar's gesture of affection and goodwill to his subject. *What will God do?* thought John.

Each of the 24 saints knew they were not worthy to receive any honor from God. They had testified with Paul, "For me to live is Christ and to die is gain." They knew they were not worthy to wear a crown in the presence of their God—even if given to them by God Himself. Then in an act of unified resolve, worshiping independently, yet acting as one, they cast their crowns at the feet of God and fell prostrate to worship Him.

"Amen," John joined them from his Patmos cave. The old apostle fell with his face to the ground, just as the elders bowed in Heaven. John prayed, "I give everything to You again." As a prisoner, John had no worldly possessions to give, yet everything the ancient apostle possessed he once again yielded to God.

He had little—a cave in which he slept; a table on which to write; paper, pen, and ink—tools he needed. These John again gave to God.

"I give You my mind," John whispered to God. It was the rededication of his mental facilities, the same thing he had done when he had first met Jesus on the seashore of Galilee.

"I give You all of my feeble strength," John voiced his re-consecration, just as he had previously given the Master all his youthful strength when he had left the nets to follow Jesus. When the 24 saints gave all to God by casting their crowns at the feet of God in Heaven, John identified with them from his vantage place on earth.

Then music began to swell in Heaven; and similar to surging waters lifting a swimmer in its tide, John was lifted by the music. The four Seraphim around the throne led all Heaven in worship, and the 24 saints joined to sing the same words. The music grew in intensity—both in volume and depth of resonance. Everyone in Heaven joined in singing...

"THOU ART WORTHY, O LORD...FOR THOU HAS CREATED ALL THINGS!"

They sang heartily for they knew God was the source of all they were and had. If God had not first created Adam, they would not have been born. If God had not preserved them on many occasions, they would have perished. If God had not redeemed them, they would have been lost. Each— joined by millions upon millions—sang as one voice...

"THOU ART WORTHY, O LORD, TO RECEIVE ALL GLORY, AND HONOR, AND POWER."

John was only supposed to gaze into Heaven so he could see the future events in order to write them down. He was only supposed to be the observer-reporter, the one who would record future events. But John could not keep silent—he was more than an observing scribe. John became a worshipper; even within the parameters of a vision, John worshiped God. His raspy voice agreed with what he heard and saw in the vision...

"THOU ART WORTHY, O LORD...BECAUSE YOU CREATED ALL THINGS. EVERYTHING WAS CREATED FOR YOUR PLEASURE AND YOUR PURPOSE."

"Yes," John agreed with the multitudes. "God is worthy because God created everything according to His purpose and His pleasure."

From John's vantage point as God's seer into Heaven, he could see all that God had created. The earth was such a small place when viewed from Heaven's perspective. The tiny earth, which had been home to millions who now live in Heaven, was small in comparison to its mammoth sun—1,300,000 times larger than the earth.

In the next galaxy, John saw a larger sun named Antares—named by God who knows all the stars by name. John could see that the burning mass of Antares was 64 million times larger than the sun of his tiny hemisphere.

Looking farther away from the earth, John saw in another constellation a larger burning star called Hercules, 100 million times larger than Antares.

Then as far as the eye could see was the burning star Epsilon, several million times larger than Hercules, flaming so bright it could be seen in all corners of God's creation. To John it seemed the farther away from earth he looked, the larger the flaming stars became—all shining to tell the people on earth the times and the seasons. God created all these things for His people on earth.

*How many stars?* John's curious mind asked. Then surveying Heaven—from one end to the other end—John could see them all in prophetic sight. The stars were too numerous for his aging mind to count, million times a million. *No*, thought John, *a billion times a billion*. Finally, he concluded, *Probably a trillion times a trillion. ...Why so many stars?*

*Because God likes stars*, John concluded. *God created them to shine for His pleasure.*

The music of Heaven interrupted John's thoughts about the stars. It was music about creation. Now, John joined the singing...

"THOU ART WORTHY, O LORD. FOR THOU HAS CREATED ALL THINGS FOR THY PLEASURE AND FOR THY PURPOSE."

## What I Learned From John's Worship

God does not need anything because He has everything; the only thing I can give to God that He doesn't already have is my praise.

I will worship God when I first enter Heaven—not look for family, friends, or anything else.

I can worship God as perfectly as angels in Heaven, because worship is measured by our sincerity, not by our perfection.

I don't deserve any rewards for anything I've done for God. All my accomplishments were completed because He motivated me and gave me the strength to do them.

I must magnify God for the greatness of His creation.

## Section Three

## Scripture: Revelation 4:1-11

Lord, John looked toward Heaven and his eyes were on an open door;
>> His ears heard Your inviting voice say,
>> "Come up here."
> Your voice penetrated the air like a trumpet.
>> You promised to show John
>> The things that will happen in the future.
> John yielded himself to the Holy Spirit,
>> Who whisked him through the open door into Heaven.
> John saw a throne in the center of Heaven,
>> And You were sitting on the throne.
> Coming from You were white rays like the flashes of a diamond
>> And red beams like the glistening of a ruby.
> There was a rainbow circling the throne
>> With a backdrop of emerald green light.

Lord, John saw 24 thrones surrounding Your throne,
>> With 24 symbolic saints sitting there.
> The saints had golden crowns on their heads,
>> And they were all dressed in white.
> John saw flashes of lightning coming from Your throne,
>> And he heard the rumble of thunder in the background.
> John saw seven burning lamps giving light,
>> Which represented the sevenfold ministry of the
>> Holy Spirit.
> John saw a sparkling crystal sea in front of Your throne;
>> There was not a ripple on its mirror-like surface.
> John saw four angels on the four corners of Your throne;
>> They looked in every direction

As they guarded Your throne.
The first looked like a lion to represent royalty;
    The second looked like an ox to represent work;
The third was like a man to symbolize humanity;
    And the fourth looked like an eagle that soars above all.

The Seraphim could see everything in all directions,
    At all times.
Day and night they worshiped God, crying out,
    "Holy...Holy...Holy, is the LORD GOD ALMIGHTY,
    Who was...Who is...and Who is to come."
Then the angels gave glory, honor, and thanks
    To You Who sits on the throne.
The 24 saints fell on their faces before You,
    Worshiping You Who lives forever.
The saints took the crowns from their heads
    And offered them in worshipful appreciation
    To You who originally rewarded them with the crowns.
The saints cried in praise, "You are worthy,
    Our Lord and God, to receive our glory, honor,
    and power."
    Then they cast their crowns at Your feet,
Because You created the earth and all the heavens;
    By Your will everything exists.
        Amen.

# Section Four

## WORSHIPING THE LAMB

### Scripture: Revelation 5:1–6:17

When John looked into Heaven, it was not like looking at a painted picture of Heaven, drawn by an artist. Rather, he entered Heaven in a prophetic presence. Even though he remained in the cave, John saw Heaven by standing on its streets, and as he twisted his ancient neck left and right, he gazed down those streets and all around. He drank in the scene with prophetic eyes. It was beautiful beyond description—the peaceful lake…the four angelic Seraphim guarding the throne…the 24 saints…and he still had to shield his eyes when he stared into the blinding light of the heavenly throne. How could he remember everything? How could he find the appropriate words to write what he saw?

Oh, and now, John was gripped with a new scene he had not previously noticed. Multitudes—not hundreds, not thousands, not millions, not billions…but more! Stretching to the endless horizon of his mind, John saw a multitude of people, almost innumerable.

John was completely unaware that the people of Heaven were not looking at him, nor were they looking at the things he saw. They all were looking at one thing, which John seemed not to notice. With his frantic endeavor to see all of Heaven, John missed a most important item. Just as a person looking at the vast seashore misses a multicolored shell lying at his feet, so John had been so blinded by the enormous number of stars in Heaven that he had missed something that was captivating everyone else.

Then John became aware that the mood in Heaven was changing. Like a classroom slowly becoming quiet because the students realize their teacher is waiting for their attention, a hushed anticipation slowly spread over all of Heaven when everyone became aware that God was waiting. John quieted his breathing as Heaven became still with anticipation. Then John saw it.

There was a scroll in the hand of the One sitting on the throne.

Squinting his weakened eyes, John saw that this was no ordinary scroll. It had seven authoritative seals to shield its message from unauthorized eyes. John had seen seals like that before. Official papers from Caesar or Roman officials always had a series of seals to make sure no unofficial person read its contents. Only the one who was supposed to receive the scroll could break its seals and read its message.

*Why hasn't God opened the scroll?* John naturally thought to himself. The apostle believed God knew everything. *God must already know what is in the scroll, and because God can do anything, He can also break the seals.*

*Why is the scroll not opened?* again John wondered.

Looking carefully at the many seals, the old apostle knew that very important papers had more than one seal. A few important Roman papers had two or more seals. The most important Roman papers had one seal for Caesar, a second seal for the Roman Senate, a third seal for the general of the army, and a fourth seal for the governor of the province.

John blinked his eyes to see more perfectly, then counted the seals. One…two…three…four…five…six…seven. The scroll in God's hand had seven seals. Seven—God's number; seven—the number of perfection. John knew the message of the scroll must be the most important message in the universe; nothing was more authoritative, for the scroll was perfectly sealed. Then a loud voice bounced off the walls of Heaven…

"WHO IS WORTHY TO BREAK THE SEALS AND OPEN THE BOOK?"

John turned to see who was speaking. He saw a strong solitary angel flying across Heaven asking the question, "WHO IS WORTHY TO OPEN AND READ THE BOOK?"

Immediately, John knew the strong angel couldn't break the seal, for he was looking for someone more worthy than himself to open the scroll. No other angel stepped forward to volunteer his services, for none of them was worthy.

John turned back to the four Seraphim guarding the throne. None of them offered to open the book. John looked up and down the row of 24 saints—neither did any of them accept the challenge. They all kept their place. No one in Heaven volunteered. Could no one open the book?

The flying angel had not asked, "Who is able?" for that question would have suggested physical ability, meaning that the seals were tough and brute strength would be needed to open the scroll. The angel had asked, "Who is worthy?" questioning if anyone had the authority to break the seals.

John thought, *What authority must a man have to be worthy to open the scroll? Must he fight better...think deep thoughts...possess more wealth...do miracles?*

John scanned the crowds of eternity past, looking for the most victorious warrior to step forth, but none was valiant enough. Not Joshua...not Samson...not David. John again looked for a wise man in history to open the seal. However, none was intelligent enough. Not Moses...not Solomon...not Abraham. Nor were any kings, prophets, priests, or miracle workers worthy to open the scroll.

Disappointedly, John began to weep. He could plainly see that God wanted the scroll opened...and he wanted what God wanted. John didn't know what would happen next, so he continued to weep silently, expecting something unexpected to happen. While it is difficult to wait for something of which you're not sure what you are waiting for, John had no other alternative—he waited. He sat on the crude chair in his cave, pulled his tunic about his chilly body, and quietly wept, in anticipation.

## Your Time to Worship

Lord, I worship You for Your infinite knowledge, for when I am frustrated by my ignorance, teach me to trust You who knows all things.

Lord, I acknowledge You who knows all things past, present, future, and things potential. Teach me to trust You who knows what is best for me.

Lord, You know everything about my feelings, desires, and hidden thoughts; teach me to trust Your purging of my ungodly thoughts and desires.

Lord, You continually know all things; teach me to trust Your plan for my life when I can't understand it, just as I know the sun is shining when I can't see it.

Lord, You are never surprised by anything; and I am shocked, disappointed, and frustrated. Teach me to trust what You know, not what I can see.

"Weep not." The silence was broken by one saint who spoke. All the eyes of Heaven focused on John tears, after they heard what was said. They knew that only John wept, for in Heaven there are no tears. John's tears of disappointment were theirs.

All the ears of Heaven listened, for they too wanted to know who was worthy to open the scroll. But even so, there were some who already knew. The one speaking knew what all the 24 saints knew, what the four angelic choir leaders knew, and what God Himself knew. They knew who could open the scroll. The speaker announced...

"THE LION OF THE TRIBE OF JUDAH IS WORTHY." John's heart leaped.

"JESUS IS WORTHY TO BREAK THE SEAL, BECAUSE HE HAS DIED FOR US. JESUS IS WORTHY TO TELL US WHAT IS IN THE SCROLL BECAUSE HE HAS BROKEN THE STRANGLEHOLD OF DEATH."

*Amen*, everyone in Heaven silently agreed.

"THE ROOT OF DAVID HAS BATTLED THE POWER OF SIN AND HAS PREVAILED," the loud voice proclaimed.

The scroll in the hand of God was the title deed to the universe. The scroll determined who owned the world and what would happen in it. And the seals were authoritative agreements by which the world's affairs were run.

The world had been God's world, because He had created it perfect; it was Paradise. The earth had glorified God, and mankind had fellow-shipped with God by walking with Him in the garden in the cool of the day. But when Adam and Eve had listened to satan, they subsequently sinned against God. Consequently, He had to judge them, and He had to judge the earth on which they lived. They then had to die, and the law of sin took control. All people aged until they died, and all died. Men lied rather than telling the truth; they became tyrants and took pleasure in harming one another; they carved idols from roots or stone, then bowed down to worship the demonic spirits that inhabited the idols.

God's Kingdom of light had been put aside for the kingdom of darkness. Thereafter, God and satan entered a contest for the souls of people, and at times it looked as if satan were prevailing through his use of the lust of the flesh, the lust of the eyes, and the appeal of selfish arrogance.

Caesar took delight in burning the apostle Paul alive on a stake in his garden, and he crucified Peter upside down. Thousands of Christians were thrown to hungry lions to be eaten alive. Why? Because satan hates God's people. But how could God allow the devil to do these things? Because life is choice, and God wants all people to freely choose to love

Him and serve Him. Those who reject God, hate God—and pour their hatred on the people of God.

But now, the end of the world has come. Now, the seals must be broken. Now, it is time for satan's power to be terminated. Now, it is time for God to take back control of the earth. Now is the time for the Kingdom of God to rule the earth.

"This is wonderful news…" John turned from the scene in Heaven to his flickering candle and parchment paper. "I must write down this good news for all who are suffering." John wanted to tell them that satan's persecution wouldn't last forever. He wanted them to know that there was a time coming when God would eliminate satan's control and reassert His own control.

As John wrote what he was hearing in Heaven, he turned again to see what was happening about the throne of God.

There was a holy hush, and those whispering were silenced by the growing stillness of the multitude. Something else was happening.

John looked in every direction to see what had captured the crowd's attention. Then the old eyes rested upon what the eyes of millions of others were observing. John saw Jesus. He knew it was Jesus because he had followed the Master for more than three years in Galilee. He had seen the resurrected Jesus in the flesh. But now John saw Him glorified.

Jesus stepped from the throne. This was not the Jesus who had lived before creation. This was not the Baby Jesus of the Bethlehem manger. This was the Jesus who had suffered as a Lamb, dying on Calvary. Every eye in Heaven saw Him as the suffering Savior; they looked at Jesus as the crucified Lamb of God. Just as each person in Heaven had individually seen Jesus in his or her conversion experience—the One who had forgiven their sin, now they were also seeing Him again in Heaven, as in the day of their salvation.

The Lamb stepped forward to the center of Heaven.

Because Jesus as the Lamb had been victorious over sin, He now in His heavenly role stepped triumphantly toward the throne. Reaching out,

Jesus took the scroll with its seven unopened seals, and because He was worthy, Jesus held the scroll high above His head. In response, the inhabitants of Heaven shouted for joy. Soon He would break the seals...but not just yet.

The four angelic Seraphim fell down in worship of Jesus, as they had worshiped the triune God on the throne. With faces to the ground, these worship leaders magnified the Lord Jesus. Then the 24 saints followed their lead. They too worshiped with their faces to the ground.

The 24 saints saw the vessels that contained all the prayers of worship, of all people, of all time—all the prayers that had ever been directed to Jesus. Taking them all—every hymn that worshiped Jesus...every prayer that exalted Jesus...every act of service that magnified Jesus...everything done in the name of Jesus—the 24 saints poured out the prayers in adoration of the Lord Jesus Christ.

All in Heaven sang a new song...new in time. Up until now, Jesus had been the Lamb who forgave their sins. Now, Jesus was also the Lamb who would terminate sin. The new song of heavenly triumph over sin, which had never been uttered until the rapture of the Church into Heaven, could now be sung. Now, at the end of the age, the new song could be sung because all believers, of all tribes, of all ages, from all the earth were gathered to witness the final victory of God over satan. So they sang a new song...

"THOU ART WORTHY TO TAKE THE BOOK AND TO BREAK THE SEALS BECAUSE YOU ARE THE LAMB WHO DIED TO REDEEM US BY YOUR BLOOD FROM OUR SINS."

John had been sitting on his wooden chair in the cave, but instinctively he dropped to his knees to cry, "Amen." He kept repeating, "Amen," for he knew his sins were many. But now John had a new reason to cry out, "Amen!" Jesus was getting ready to finish sin and the devil forever. "Do so quickly," John prayed.

### Your Time to Worship

Lord, I love to sing about Your mercy, but I'm afraid of Your judgment. Bury my sin in the blood of the Lamb.

Lord, I would devote myself to sin, if I did not know You punish misbehavior. Lord, make me obey You.

Lord, there is "straightness" in your expectations, but I am "crooked"! Draw a straight line with this crooked stick that I call life.

Lord, You have never condemned an innocent person, nor have You overlooked the guilty. Remember, I come to You in the perfection of Jesus Christ; He is all I plead.

Lord, You never delight in making people miserable for the sake of misery, but You punish because of Your truth. I worship You in the security of Jesus Christ.

Jesus took the book from God and stepped to the center of Heaven. Soon there'd be no more aging...no more persecution...no more tears...no more death. Jesus had the future of the universe in His hand and soon, everything would be light.

John's mind went back to those martyrs torn to bits by lions; soon it would be all right. John remembered his parishioners outside the front of the cave praying for him, separated from loved ones, starving and suffering. Soon it would be all right for them. For all the persecutions that Christians have endured for Christ, soon it would be all right.

As Jesus stood in the center of Heaven with the book in His hand, John looked around to see everyone worshiping Him. John saw multitudes of angels worshiping Jesus the Lamb; those perfect messengers were each crying out, "HOLY, HOLY, HOLY."

*How many?* he wondered.

In his limited estimate, John thought there must be ten thousand times ten thousand, plus thousands of thousands. So many they staggered his mind.

"I can't count them," he gasped.

Then beyond the angels, John saw every person who ever believed in Jesus up to that date, plus those who would believe in Jesus in the future. John saw them all with his prophetic eye. Even though he was imprisoned in a cave and trapped on a tiny island ten miles by six miles, John saw the future for which he prayed. He saw in a vision all believers of all time surrounding the throne of God.

From the drab limitations of a cave in the rocks, John saw the glories of Heaven. He tried to grasp how many followers of Jesus were there—millions times millions. Black-skinned believers of Africa; brown-skinned believers of India; fair-skinned ones of Greece, Italy, and Spain. They came from the East—Chinese, Japanese, and from the islands of the sea. They all spoke a different language, but together they sang the same words...

"WORTHY...." Their music was awesome as they sang, "WORTHY IS THE LAMB."

From the cave on Patmos, John joined in singing, "Worthy."

The entire host of Heaven sang in unison, "HE IS WORTHY BECAUSE HE WAS SLAIN FOR US." They worshiped the One on the throne and the Lamb, "HE IS WORTHY TO RECEIVE OUR PRAISE...OUR RICHES...OUR ALL."

Then suddenly, Heaven was silent, a silence that demanded attention. John rose from his crude chair in the cave. After standing with those in Heaven, he dared not move. The moment was filled with anticipation. John knew what he wanted to do...he knew what everyone in Heaven wanted to do. Then with no one giving a signal to begin, and no one wait-ing, John in the cave along with everyone in Heaven, all responded at the same time and sang the timeless hymn that would be written centuries later, "O COME LET US ADORE HIM."

### What I Learned About the Lamb

I must always remember to look past my difficulties to the joy of seeing Jesus in Heaven.

I must make Jesus the center of my focus on earth, because He will be the center of my focus in Heaven.

I must constantly worship Jesus for the salvation He accom-plished for me on Calvary. If I lose the focus of sins forgiven, I've lost my perspective in life.

I can endure difficulties on earth, knowing Jesus will one day do away with all evil and its influence in the future.

I find purpose and meaning in life when I worship Jesus, the One who is worthy to receive my adoration.

## Section Four

## Scripture: Revelation 5:1–6:17

Lord, John saw a scroll in Your right hand;
>There was writing on both sides of each page,
>And it was officially sealed with seven seals.
John saw a mighty angel who asked with a loud voice,
>"Who is worthy to open the seal and open the scroll?"
No one was worthy in Heaven, or on earth, or in hell
>To open and read what was in the scroll.
John wept bitterly because no one could open the scroll;
>But one of the saints on one of the 24 thrones said,
>"Do not weep; there is One who is worthy."
Only Jesus, the Lion of the tribe of Judah, and
>The root of David
>Is worthy to break the seven seals of the scroll,
Because Jesus has triumphed over satan
>Who once ruled the universe of souls.
John saw Jesus the Lamb, standing next to Your throne,
>Standing between the Seraphim guarding the throne
>And the 24 saints sitting on 24 thrones.
The Lamb, Jesus, had been sacrificed.
>All Your wrath had been satisfied.
>The whole work of salvation—"It is finished."
The Lamb, Jesus, took the scroll out of Your hand.
>Then the four seraphim bowed to Jesus,
>Followed by the 24 saints who also bowed.
Each one sang worship to the Lamb.
>Then they poured out all the worship praise
>Of all believers, of all time.
Then they sang a new song,

"You are worthy to take the scroll
And break the seals to open the scroll,
Because the sacrifice of Your blood,
Purchased salvation for all people,
Of every language, from every tribe, and from every nation.
You have made them priests to intercede
And serve in Your Kingdom."

Lord, in John's vision he heard the music
Of an innumerable choir of angels
Gathered around Your throne.
John said there were ten thousand times ten thousand angels,
Plus thousands upon thousands who were shouting,
"The Lamb who was sacrificed is worthy to open the seals,
For He has power, wisdom, riches,
Strength, honor, blessings, and glory."
Then John heard worship from everything that has breath—
Everything in Heaven, everything that lives on earth,
And in the seas and even hell itself.
They worshiped You sitting on the throne,
And Jesus who had the scroll in His hand,
Saying, "All praise, honor, power, and glory
To You and to the Lamb."
And the four guarding Seraphim and the 24 saints
Also worshiped saying, "Amen!"

*The First Seal*

Lord, John saw the Lamb break the first seal,
And unroll the scroll.
Then one of the four Seraphim
With a voice sounding like thunder shouted, "Come!"
John saw a white horse, and the rider
Was holding only a bow—no arrows.

The rider was given a victor's crown,
>And he went from one battle to another.

## The Second Seal

When Jesus broke the second seal,
>Another Seraphim shouted, "Come!"
John saw a second horse who was bright red.
>The rider was given a huge sword and commanded,
>"And take peace from the earth and set people
>to slaughter one another."

## The Third Seal

When Jesus broke the third seal,
>Another Seraphim shouted, "Come!"
John saw a black horse, and its rider
>Held a pair of scales to measure things.
The Seraphim cried, "A loaf of bread,
>Or three pounds of barley for forty dollars;
>There is no oil or wine available anywhere."

## The Fourth Seal

When Jesus broke the fourth seal,
>A fourth Seraphim cried, "Come out!"
John saw a sickly pale horse, and its rider
>Was named Plague;
>Hell was snatching up all who died.
A fourth of the earth's population was killed
>By Plague, by war, by famine,
>By disease, and by wild animals.

## The Fifth Seal

When Jesus broke the fifth seal,
>John saw under an altar

All those who had been martyred for witnessing Your Word,
　And being faithful in holy living.
The martyrs cried to You, "How much longer
　　Will You wait before taking vengeance
　　On those who have killed us?"
Each martyr was given a white robe of righteousness
　　And told to rest until the coming judgment,
Because there would continue to be martyrs
　　Until the second coming of Christ,
　　Who would be killed just as they did.

*The Sixth Seal*

When Jesus broke the sixth seal,
　　There was a violent earthquake and the sun didn't shine;
　　Darkness covered the earth.
The stars began to fall like figs dropping from a tree
　　When a wind storm shakes it;
　　Everything was pitch black.
The mountains and islands of the sea
　　Shifted their original locations.
Everyone panicked and hid themselves in caves.
　　Kings, government leaders, military commanders,
　　Rich and poor—all people tried to hide.
They cried for the rocks to cover and hide them
　　From the wrath of the Lamb,
　　Because they wouldn't survive Your coming judgment.
　　　　Amen.

# Section Five

## Martyrs Worship as They Enter Heaven, and The Seven Trumpet-Judgments

### Scripture: Revelation 7:1–11:15

The aged John had been so focused on seeing the Lamb standing at the center of Heaven, he forgot everything else. He forgot Rome was persecuting Christians. He forgot he was a prisoner on Patmos. He forgot the damp cave and the aches in his decrepit body. He forgot his flock waiting for him outside the cave. Nothing else matters when you look at Jesus.

As Jesus held high the scroll, the title deed to Heaven that no one else could open, the seals seemed more compelling than the book itself. In the next instant, without effort, Jesus broke the seals. It did not take supernatural ability to break the seals; they were simply wax seals that could be broken with the flip of a small finger. John had sealed many letters in his life with melted wax from a candle. Then to make sure the recipient knew he was the one who had sent the document, John had pressed his signet ring in the warm wax. After the wax hardened, his seal—the family signet—guaranteed his authorship. No one else could reproduce the seal without his signet ring.

*Who sealed the book Jesus is holding?* John asked himself.

John was so focused on Jesus breaking the seals in Heaven that he missed the judgment that was being poured out on earth in the meantime. The rapture had come, saints were in Heaven, and the Tribulation was being poured out on mankind. Satan had been "the god of this world," but now God would purify the earth from his domination.

From the beginning, satan had tempted the earth's inhabitants to follow him, using the love of money, the pleasure of the flesh, and the pride of life. Satan's dominant power on earth had been the influence of a worldly system that conquered the lives of humans.

When the first seal was broken, John saw an angel leave the presence of God riding a white horse. The rider had been commissioned to take peace from the hearts of the people. As the white horse galloped across the face of the earth, everyone was gripped by fear of war; even rumors of coming war stole peace from the hearts of people far from the battle zones. Because the people of the earth had rejected the peace of God, He was sending them the alternative—agony and misery. Usually punishment does not hurt as much as the anticipation of punishment, just as fear of war is probably worse than war itself.

When the second seal was broken, John saw a second angel on a red horse leave the presence of God. *What judgment will He deliver?* thought John. The rider on the red horse instigated war on earth—brother against brother—nation against nation. Men were hacked to pieces with swords, the ground was soaked with blood, millions of widows were grieving.

Why would God send war? God began cleansing the earth of sin by giving it more sin and its consequences than anyone ever anticipated. The rewards of iniquity cause men to hate iniquity. Men cry out, "My sin is greater than I can bear." God allows unparalleled slaughter on battlefields because hell is punished by hell itself. Wars are the tools of satan used to capture his prey. Wars are fought for the love of money, to gain things that satisfy the flesh, and for the pride of rulers and nations.

There was so much carnage that strong men became weak; they vomited and shook with fear. However, rather than repenting of sin, the bloodied soldiers cursed God with clenched fists. Rather than turn to God for peace, men sought to end violence with more violence.

The punishment from God demonstrates the law of God. Those who reject God in peace, hate God all the more when judged by war. Because they won't turn to God in war or peace, the Lawgiver must demonstrate

His control, punishing the lawbreaker by immersing him in lawless anguish.

When the third seal was broken, John saw a third angel ride out of Heaven on a black horse—another messenger of judgment—on his way to judge the earth. This angel spread hunger, famine, and deathly starvation to the earth.

Corresponding judgments were already taking its toll on the earth itself. Forest fires burning out of control created voluminous black clouds that blocked the rays of life-giving sunlight. Growing things began to die. Then, because there was nothing to eat, animals died. Food disappeared from stores; rationing occurred followed by empty shelves and pantries. Rioting broke out. Malnourished children died first, then the aged, and finally the strong.

John didn't want to witness the next scene. Since the first time he had looked into Heaven, the aged apostle turned away from the vision and looked around his desolate cave. He saw the white cloth covering the morsel of bread on the table. His meager diet on Patmos didn't look so small in comparison to the coming world starvation. John wept for those who would die slowly of hunger.

Then John looked again at the vision to see the fourth seal broken from the scroll. He saw another angel leave Heaven riding on a sickly pale horse—the judgment of death. People died by all means, including starvation. Animals that had once feared man, now starving, were attacking mankind for food. All those who had rejected God to seek "pleasure for a season" and had enjoyed instant gratification, now feared the death predator that stalked them. Their original rejection of God justified His punishment for them, for even in their day of dread, they did not turn to Him.

The breaking of the fifth seal revealed God's people who were suffering along with the unsaved. The judgments of God fell not only on unbelievers, but on many who believed in God. Some believers were killed with guns, others were burned at the stake, some were martyred publicly, and still others just disappeared from the public eye. Because the entire earth was being judged, God's people died along with those who hated Him. God's people suffered just as much as the unsaved. The only difference was the attitude of their hearts. The unsaved hated God for their suffering and cursed God with clenched fists. The believers bowed their heads to pray,

"How long, Oh Lord? How long?"

Those on the earth who were martyred were given white robes. They were told, "Rest from your labors till others join you, for more will be martyred." They were promised that suffering on earth would end shortly.

The goodness of God, which allows rain to fall upon the just and the unjust, also allows His judgment to afflict the saved and unsaved alike. Both are killed in earthquakes, pestilence, and famine. Those who reject God in this life will reject Him in death. Those born with clenched fists will die with clenched fists, defying God who gave them life, cursing God for allowing them to die. Then from eternal flames, their blackened eyes will stare defiantly, only to eternally reject God time and again. A look into the hearts of those judged will vindicate God's judgment. While the unsaved curse God from hell, saved people will continue to pray...

"How long?..."

God does not enjoy punishing anyone, but having established laws in the Garden of Eden, He must do what the law demands. Because life is choice, God allows all to choose the filthiness of sin, if they so desire; then during the Tribulation, God will give them what they have chosen. He will allow them to be filthy still. They will cry out, "I cannot bear the filthiness of my sin." They will not cry for God to save them, for if they repented, God would redeem them. No one in hell will ever cry for God to let them out. The choice they made in life to reject God is the same choice they will continue to make in hell. They will declare, "We will not have this man Jesus rule over us," and they will eternally reject God.

The aged John wept as he saw the collapse of civilization. He loved people, and as "the beloved disciple," love broke his heart. The vision of the future tore his heart apart. God was pouring His retribution out on the earth, beginning to cleanse it for a new day—a new people—a new age to come.

When the sixth seal on the title deed to Heaven was broken, a great earthquake shook the earth, more violent than any previous measurement on the Richter Scale. Buildings fell upon their inhabitants. Rocks tumbled down mountains and crushed villages. Great cracks in the earth swallowed up those running to safety. John thought dying by starvation had been terrible, but now, it seemed as though everyone and everything—bridges, towers, factories, churches—were being destroyed. The stars created by God came hurling to earth, causing forest fires, tidal waves, and toxic vapors, killing thousands more.

Presidents and army generals knew the end was near and that God was judging the earth. Yet, rather than praying to God, they ran to hide in caves from the natural disasters and prayed to the rocks...

"Fall on us to hide us from the face of the Lamb who is coming to judge us."

## Your Time to Worship

Lord, You give the devil and his followers what they continually seek—ruin, disaster, and misery. Thank You for giving me peace.

Lord, when I see human devastation, You are there working Your plan. Thank You for taking care of me.

Lord, when it seems satan is controlling everything, You are behind the scenes, directing Your plan. Thank You for working all things for good to us who love You.

Lord, when I have personal catastrophes, You do not let them overwhelm me. Thank You for protecting me.

Lord, when the lives of good people are destroyed by satan, You have a greater life and reward for them in Heaven. Thank You for Your faithfulness to each one of us who follow You.

John looked back into Heaven and saw four angels holding back the winds of the earth, refusing to allow the gentle refreshing breezes blow through the meadows. Nor did the storms blow across the face of the ocean that would ultimately bring rain for the farmers. Without the wind, the heat became unbearable on the remaining population already reeling from God's judgment. Without the wind, there was no pollination, and plants couldn't reproduce. Birds didn't fly, nor was there rainfall from Heaven to cool the searing heat. And without rain, the ground cracked, and vegetation died.

Why is it that people never appreciate the wind, until it refuses to blow? Why is it that people never praise God for good things, until they are taken away? When there was no wind to hold things together, life came unglued.

Suddenly, John heard a loud voice from Heaven, "DO NOT HURT THE EARTH BY WITHHOLDING THE WIND." The voice explained, "WHEN YOU WITHHOLD THE WIND, YOU HURT THE SEA, THE TREES, AND ALL LIFE ON EARTH."

As John listened to the voice, he knew there was grace in the judgment of God. The strong voice was heard again...

"DON'T HURT THE EARTH UNTIL GOD HAS SEALED HIS SER-VANTS, FOR SOME BELIEVERS WILL NOT DIE. THEY WILL LIVE THROUGH THE JUDGMENT AS A TESTIMONY TO ME UPON THIS EARTH."

They represented every tribe of Israel who came from every place on earth; they represented God's people who were yet to serve Him upon the face of the earth.

Every unsaved person was branded with a seal on their forehead or hand. It was the number 666, the number of man; and those with the number 666 claimed that they belonged to satan, not to God.

In contrast, God's servants were given the brand sign of God in their foreheads. They were sealed with the name of God, a sign of His ownership. These were those who would live for God but would be martyred during the Tribulation.

## Entrance Into Heaven

A visionary light turned John's eyes toward Heaven. He saw a light beam, like a vast swinging bridge, extending upward from the earth through a field of fire. It was a shining path that reached into Heaven. Upon it, a vast throng of saints marched triumphantly toward the city of light. John tried to count the number—too great to determine—entering Heaven. In the parade were aged gray-headed saints...teenagers...entire families...children barely able to walk...and babies in arm. They were the martyrs who had been slaughtered for the cause of Jesus Christ upon the face of the earth. They came from every people group on earth—from Korea, Africa—brown faces, white faces, and those with yellow skin. They spoke every tongue, and yet in their differences they could communicate with one another, both hearing and understanding what others said.

John leaned forward to observe them closer. Did he know them? Were any of the 12 apostles there?

They were marching, one group behind the other...orderly...with great dignity...accountable...respectable. John knew he would not join them because Jesus had said he would die a natural death, not a martyr's death. But regardless, John respected them and wanted to march with them—not because of their violent death, but because of their consecration. They had given all.

Each smiled with the look of contentment, yet their altered faces still shown shock. They had learned from their death experience, and maturity remained even in their glorification. The virtue of their character shone through their countenance. John couldn't forget what they had experienced; he would always remember their dedication.

Each martyr in the parade was wearing a white robe symbolizing purity. These people had not dipped their colors, nor had they compromised their stand for God. They had come out of the Great Tribulation having washed their robes, made pure in the blood of Jesus Christ.

"Awesome!" John exclaimed as he saw them triumphantly entering Heaven. As a lad in Jerusalem, he had seen the Roman legions entering the Eternal City dressed in battle gear—their symbols of victory on parade. But Roman pomp couldn't now compare to this spectacular sight that John was witnessing.

The great multitude continued to come, drawn by an irresistible force that pulled them into the very center of Heaven where the throne of God was located. They all wanted to see the One for whom they had paid the ultimate price. They wanted to see God the Father and the Lamb. They had suffered for Him, now they wanted to worship Him.

Just as on Palm Sunday, the multitudes had gone out from Jerusalem to meet Jesus, waving palm branches in their hands, a symbol of victory, so these people in Heaven waved palm branches shouting the same praise...

"HOSANNA...HOSANNA...HOSANNA...!"

They approached the center of Heaven, the throne of God, shining as the sun; however, it was impossible to see God, just as it is impossible to look into the brightness of the sun.

And at the four corners of the throne of God were the guarding Seraphim, the worship leaders still there, directing everyone in worship and calling all voices to magnify the One who sat upon the throne.

In front of the throne were the 24 saints, some of whom had also died a martyr's death, just like the symbolic crowd of 144,000 who had paid the ultimate price of love to Him who sat upon the throne. Seeing the vast number of martyrs entering Heaven, the 24 saints fell upon their faces to worship God. Then one of the saints asked, "Who are these who are dressed in white clothes, and where have they come from?"

"You know the answer to that," John said to him. "These are the martyrs who have come out of the Great Tribulation. Their sins have been washed away in the blood of Jesus Christ and now they have come to worship God."

As the martyrs faithfully served God by dying on earth, now they would serve God by worshiping Him in Heaven. Then they joined in with the four angelic worship leaders and the 24 saints to sing...

"BLESSING...AND GLORY...AND WISDOM...AND THANKSGIVING...AND HONOR...AND POWER...AND MIGHT...TO THE ONE WHO SITS ON THE THRONE."

John remembered the sevenfold blessings when he had first observed Heaven. These martyrs were now repeating the same sevenfold blessings of God. *This worship must come deep from within the heart of the people,* John thought. Then he picked up his pen to write again...

"BLESSING...BE TO GOD FOREVER AND EVER."

John agreed with them, saying, "Amen."

"GLORY...BE TO GOD FOREVER AND EVER."

"Amen," repeated John.

"WISDOM...BE TO GOD FOREVER AND EVER."

"Amen," echoed from the cave.

"THANKSGIVING...BE TO GOD FOREVER AND EVER."

"Amen."

"HONOR...BE TO GOD FOREVER AND EVER."

"Amen."

"POWER...BE TO GOD FOREVER AND EVER."

"Amen."

"MIGHT...BE TO GOD FOREVER AND EVER."

"Amen and Amen."

Those who are martyrs have a special place in the heart of God. Because they have died for Him, the Lamb will dwell among them with His special presence. Never again will they hunger, neither will they thirst. They will not remember suffering from lack of food and water. God will wipe away every painful memory. Never again will they suffer from the scorching heat of the sun, nor will anything hurt them.

The Lamb will constantly feed them and will lead them to living fountains of water. And for every pain—and remembrance of pain—the Lamb shall wipe away every tear.

---

### Your Time to Worship

Lord, You are so full of surprises; when I fear death, You give me life and a parade. Thank You for caring.

Lord, Your surprises come unexpectedly; when I expect bad days, You give me a good eternity. Thank You for life.

Lord, You told me to keep my lamp trimmed because You might come at any hour. Thank You for keeping promises.

Lord, You surprised the scoffers of Noah's day by sending a flood, but You did what You promised. Thank You for Your faithfulness.

Lord, You gave talents to Your workers and told them to work faithfully till You returned. When payday came, You rewarded them. Thank You for rewards promised to me in the future.

---

At length the parade was over, and the last martyr entered the doors of Heaven. The singing—hallelujah singing on key—had faded to John's ear.

Then John turned away from the vision and made his way slowly back to the flickering candle on the table. What time was it?...

Then the cricket choruses of the evening filled his ears. The night approached and urged him to get busy writing what he had seen. But before he wrote...just once more...John had to worship God...

"Thank You for strength against the approaching night...thank You for the serenade of the crickets...thank You for the melodious voices of martyrs climbing through the starry fields to Heaven...thank You for the shouts of hallelujah!"

## What I Learned From the Martyrs' Parade

I will enjoy in Heaven the benefits of the decisions I make on earth.

I should be happy to identify with God's cause on earth, because I will receive His mark on my forehead in Heaven.

I should praise God for everything—even sufferings—because God will reward me for them when I get to Heaven.

I should do all I can to win people to Christ on earth because there will be no second chance of salvation after death.

I should not blame God for my suffering because tribulation will come to all—both saved and unsaved.

I know God loves me and will preserve me, while satan's desire is to destroy all people.

## Section Five

### Scripture: Revelation 7:1–11:15

Lord, John saw four angels holding back the wind
      To prevent it from blowing on land or sea.
    Next, John saw another angel coming from the sunrise,
      Carrying the seals of God.
    A voice cried, "Seal the servants of God first
      Before you do any damage on land or sea."
    Then John heard there were 144,000 sealed
      Jews who came from all the tribes of Israel;
    Twelve thousand came from each tribe—from Judah, Reuben,
      Gad, Asher, Naphtali, Manasseh, Simeon,
      Levi, Issachar, Zebulun, Joseph, and Benjamin.
    In addition to the 144,000, John saw another great multitude
      From every race, language, and nation,
    Standing before You and Jesus, the Lamb,
      Wearing white robes and holding palm branches.
      They cried out in worship,
    "Salvation comes from You who sits upon the throne
      And from the Lamb who died for us."
    Then the angels formed a huge circle around
      The 24 saints and the four Seraphim.
    The angels bowed to the ground and worshiped,
      "Amen...praise and glory and wisdom
      And thanks and power and strength
      Be to You our God forever and ever. Amen!"

Lord, one of the saints asked John, "Who are these
      Dressed in white robes?
      Where did they come from?"

John asked the Lord Jesus to tell him
> Who these people were. Jesus said,
"These are the martyrs who were killed
> In the Great Tribulation;
Therefore, their robes are washed in
> The blood of the Lamb."
Now they stand in front of God's throne to
> Worship Him day and night.
The Lamb will take care of them
> So they will never hunger nor thirst,
> Nor suffer anything, ever again.
The Lamb will satisfy their needs for food,
> And will quench their need for water,
> And You will wipe away any remembrance of pain or suffering.

*The Seventh Seal*

After this parenthetical view of the martyrs in the Tribulation,
> All eyes in Heaven focused on the Lamb
> As He broke the final seal on the scroll.
There was great silence in Heaven as the Lamb
> Prepared to return to the earth;
> It was time for the Second Coming of Christ.

The seven seals describe events on earth during the coming seven-year Tribulation period. The (last) seventh seal judgment describes the event when Christ returns to judge the world. Next, the seven trumpets will sound. Similar to one leaf of cabbage covering another, the trumpets describe judgmental events during the Tribulation that happen simultaneously with the seven seals, but from a different perspective. The (last) seventh trumpet describes the Second Coming of Christ, including the same events as the seventh seal. Finally, there are seven bowls of judgment (see Rev. 16:1-21). Again, like one leaf of lettuce covers the other leaves, the bowl judgments occur simultaneously with the seals and trumpet judgments. The last bowl judgment describes the battle of Armageddon and the Second Coming of Christ.

Lord, seven angels stood before You,
>> And You gave them seven trumpets.
>> Then You told them to be prepared
>>> To announce judgments coming to the earth.
>> Another angel went to the altar in Heaven
>>> With a large amount of incense
>> To mix with the prayers of God's people,
>>> To offer to You who sits upon the throne,
>> The sweet smelling fragrance of prayers
>>> That ascends up to worship You.
>> When the angel threw fire from the altar to the earth,
>>> Thunder rumbled, lightning crashed,
>>> And an earthquake shook the earth.
>> Then the seven angels with seven trumpets
>>> Prepared to blow their message of coming judgment.

*The First Trumpet*

Lord, when the first angel blew his trumpet,
>> Hail and fire rained down on the earth.
>> One third of the earth was set on fire where
>>> One third of the trees and green grass was burnt up.

*The Second Trumpet*

Lord, when the second angel blew his trumpet,
>> Something like a great mountain of fire

Was dropped into the oceans.
One third of the water was polluted as with blood.
One third of the living things in the oceans
And one third of the ships were destroyed.

*The Third Trumpet*

Lord, when the third angel blew his trumpet,
A huge burning star named Wormwood,
Fell on a third of all the rivers and streams.
The waters became bitter as persimmons
So that many people died who drank the water.

*The Fourth Trumpet*

Lord, when the fourth angel blew his trumpet,
A third of the sun quit shining,
And light from a third of the stars went out.
Daylight was shortened by one third,
And the night was blacker than usual.

Lord, John saw an angel like an eagle fly over Heaven
Announcing, "Woe…woe…woe to the
Inhabitants of the earth."
The next three trumpet judgments
Will be much worse than the original four.

*The Fifth Trumpet*

Lord, the fifth angel blew his trumpet;
One of God's servants that came from Heaven to earth
Had the keys to the bottomless pit.
Smoke poured out of it when it was unlocked,
So the sun and sky were darkened.
The smoke spawned locust-demons,
And they spread where the smoke blew.

The locust-demons attacked people
    Who didn't have God's seal on their foreheads.
The sting didn't kill anyone, but
    Gave constant pain like a scorpion's sting.
People wanted to die,
    But death escaped them.
The locust-demons looked like horses armed for battle
    Having faces that looked human,
With crowns on their heads, and women's hair,
    And teeth like lion's teeth.
They wore body armor as strong as steel,
    And the noise of their wings sounded like
    The charge of horses and chariots into battle.
Their tails stung like a scorpion,
    And the sores they left ached for five months.
The king of them was the angel from the bottomless pit,
    Whose Hebrew name is Abaddon,
    And his Greek name is Apollyon.

*The Sixth Trumpet*

Lord, when the sixth angel blew his trumpet,
    John heard a voice from the altar before the throne,
    Saying, "Release the four demons kept captive
    Beyond the Euphrates River for this hour.
    They will kill a third of the remaining population of the Earth."
Then John heard it said,
    There were 200,000 locust-warriors.
John saw the locust-demons like riders on horses.
    Some had red armor, others had blue armor,
    And the color of the rest was yellow.
The horses looked as if they had lion heads.
    Smoke, fire, and brimstone blew from their mouths,
    Killing one third of the remaining population.

Their power was in their mouth and tail,
>Their tails were like snakes
>That were able to kill with their bite.
The population of the world that escaped their wrath
>Did not repent of their evil,
Nor did they stop worshiping demon-idols
>Made of gold, silver, bronze, stone, and wood—
>Idols that can't see, hear, or walk.
Nor did they quit murdering, stealing,
>Committing sexual sins, or practicing witchcraft.

Revelation 10:1–11:14 are a parenthesis in the unfolding drama of the Tribulation. John sees an angel that has seven thunder judgments, but they are so terrible, John is told not to write them in his book. Then John describes some of the events that happen in the first part of the Tribulation in Jerusalem.

Lord, John saw another mighty angel come down from Heaven,
>Surrounded by a cloud
>With a rainbow about his head.
The angel's face shined like the sun, his feet like fire.
>He had in his hand a small open book.
He planted his right foot in the oceans
>And his left foot on land.
He shouted louder than a roaring lion.
>Then seven thunder-judgments rolled across Heaven.
John was prepared to write what he saw
>When a voice stopped him saying,

"Keep secret the message of the seven thunder-judgments;
    Do not write them down."
The angel standing in the oceans and on the land
    Lifted his right hand to Heaven
And swore by You Who lives forever,
        You who created all of Heaven
        And everything on the earth.
The time of waiting is over; Jesus will come
        When the seventh angel blows his trumpet.
        Then Your secret intentions will be fully realized.

Lord, John heard a heavenly voice telling him to get the little book.
        So John asked the angel to give it to him.
The angel said, "Read it as you would devour a meal;
        It will upset your stomach,
        But it will be sweet as you eat it."
As John read the book, the angel's words came true.
        It tasted sweet as honey, but it turned his stomach sour.
The book contained a message for John to preach and write,
        A message of what will happen in the Tribulation
        To rulers, people, ethnic groups, and nations.

Lord, John was given a measuring stick and told to
        Go measure the Temple in Jerusalem, the altar,
        And find out how many people worship there.
John was told not to measure the outer court
        Because Gentiles gather there,
        And they will destroy the Temple after 42 months.

You promised to send two witnesses—Enoch and Elijah—
from Heaven,
        Because they did not die on earth,
        Who preached for 1,260 days in Jerusalem.
They came as the fulfillment of the two olive trees
        And the two lamps which stood before Your throne.[1]

When enemies attacked these two, they were able
>   To do judgment-miracles
>   To destroy their enemies.
They prayed so that it would not rain,
>   And they turned water into blood,
>   And sent plagues—as did Moses—on their enemies.
After three and a half years, the Antichrist
>   Came from the bottomless pit to fight them
>   And finally killed them.

Their corpses were left in the main street of Jerusalem
>   So unsaved people could see they were dead
>   And put their trust in the Antichrist.
People from every nation, ethnic group, and language
>   Saw their bodies for three and a half days.

The unsaved rejoiced thinking their torment was over
>   And the suffering caused by the Tribulation was past.
The nonbeliever celebrated and gave presents to everyone,
>   Thinking these two who had brought plagues on the world
>   Were now dead and their troubles were over.

Lord, after three and a half days
>   You breathed life into the two witnesses.
Just as everyone had seen their dead bodies,
>   Now everyone saw them being raised from the dead.
Then a loud voice shouted, "COME UP HERE!"
>   They went to Heaven as their enemies watched.
Immediately, a violent earthquake shook Jerusalem,
>   A tenth of the city was destroyed,
>   And seven thousand people died in the earthquake.
Those who lived in Jerusalem—the Jews—were fearful,
>   And began praising You, the God of Heaven.

Lord, the seventh angel blew his trumpet
>> And Heaven got ready for Christ's return to earth.
>> Amen.

## Endnote

1. See Zechariah 4:1-14

# Section Six

# WORSHIP: WHEN WE FIRST SEE THE ARK, AND THE SEVEN PERSONAGES OF THE FUTURE TRIBULATION

## Scripture: Revelation 11:15–13:18

Each time John saw another vision, it was as though the drab walls of his cave became a giant painting of future events. And what John witnessed, he described quickly in writing, trusting nothing to memory. Through his tear-filled eyes, he then dutifully took his quill and scratched what he saw into letters. The words became alive on the page, and page after page told the story of judgment on earth. Finally, when John could endure the judgment no longer, God would pull back the curtains of Heaven to reveal the occupants worshiping God. Just as a fresh tiny violet, growing out of the ashes of a blackened forest ravaged by fire, signifies hope and a new beginning, so was John's spirit refreshed each time he saw people worshiping in Heaven.

Six trumpets had sounded, each announcing the next severe judgment. A trumpet was a familiar sound to John. On many occasions, he had heard a trumpet calling Roman soldiers to duty, and as a boy, he had learned the meaning of each different trumpet blast.

John had also been taught the importance of the Jewish trumpets calling Israel to worship in the Temple. He knew the Old Testament story of over a million Israelites wandering 40 years in the wilderness, directed by a trumpet blast. Each trumpet call had indicated a different direction to the people.

Now, during the Tribulation, God sent angels to announce judgments with trumpet sounds. Six times the trumpet had blared out its call of judgment, and John was waiting for the seventh. Would the final trumpet call for the most severe judgment?

Unexpectedly, when the seventh angel sounded his trumpet across the corridors of Heaven, there were no judgments handed down. Rather, the door to Heaven began to open. Similar to a Roman trumpet signaling the opening of the gates to a city, so the seventh trumpet indicated it was time for Heaven to open.

Once more, John was transported from his cave on Patmos into the presence of God, as he looked into Heaven and heard many loud voices crying out…

"THE KINGDOMS OF THIS WORLD ARE BECOME THE KINGDOMS OF OUR LORD AND OF HIS CHRIST, AND JESUS SHALL REIGN FOREVER AND EVER."

Once again. the four angelic worship leaders around the throne led Heaven in praising God. When they fell on their faces to worship the Lord, they motivated all Heaven to join them, including the 24 saints.

While judgments were being poured out on the earth, all those in Heaven were worshiping God. They were not celebrating the punishment of their enemy, nor were there joyous feelings of vindication or revenge. Rather, everyone was focusing on God and the Lamb.

Punishment, however, is necessary for lawbreakers. God's perfect law cannot allow one act of rebellion to go unnoticed, nor can disobedience be overlooked. A rebel cannot break the law of God without it eventually breaking him. Many lawbreakers think that because they are not immediately judged, God is weak or He doesn't care. But God doesn't judge broken laws instantaneously. The patience of God gives all time to repent. The goodness of God gives to everyone a window of opportunity. Payday does not come every time a person sins, but it will come someday…assuredly…convincingly…and deadly.

The worship leaders cried, "WE GIVE YOU THANKS, LORD GOD ALMIGHTY…WHO WAS ALWAYS LORD IN THE PAST…WHO IS

LORD OF THE PRESENT...AND WHO WILL ALWAYS BE LORD IN THE AGES TO COME."

John looked into the faces of the people worshiping God and heard their voices exalting Him as their Lord and Master. Then the people cried...

"WE PRAISE YOU BECAUSE NOW THROUGH YOUR JUDGMENTS, YOUR GREAT POWER REIGNS OVER THE EARTH."

For centuries, satan had enjoyed his limited rebellion on earth. He rejoiced when David sinned with Bathsheba to spoil God's honor. He rejoiced when Peter denied Jesus three times. The demons of hell laughed when churches were burned and missionaries were martyred. They delighted to see godly people suffer persecution, thieves break into the homes of Christians to steal their livelihood, and believers hanging on a cross just as their Lord had done.

Satan rejoiced when Christians were addicted to sin, and he only grudgingly gave up those who became free in Christ.

But where was God when His people had suffered?

Why hadn't He immediately rushed in to stop violence against Christians, or to prevent death, or to protect His people? Because the scroll had been sealed with seven seals; the title deed to the earth had been wrapped up in legal litigation. Satan had his day in court. As "the god of this world," he was allowed limited victories.

At times, God did intervene for His followers in answer to prayer—to protect His children. At other times, satan had been defeated because of the faith of God's servants. But the earth had been satan's domain. Some had even called this planet "the playground of the devil." Now, God was taking it back by purifying the earth through tribulation and judgment.

The four worship leaders around the throne cried out thanksgiving to God. The 24 saints joined them, and millions upon millions of voices flooded Heaven, like a river rushing down a valley to the sea. They all were singing...

"THOU HAS TAKEN BACK THE EARTH TO REIGN. THOU HAS MANIFESTED YOUR POWER OVER THE EARTH!"

Satan would not give up easily, however; rebels would not roll over in submission to God. When the powerful hand of God fell upon the earth during the Tribulation, those in rebellion did not cry out for forgiveness, but intensified their rebellion against God. At the same time, the worshippers of Heaven continued to sing to God…

"WHEN YOU ARE TAKING BACK THE EARTH, THE NATIONS ARE ANGRY BECAUSE OF YOUR WRATH. THE NATIONS ARE ANGRY BECAUSE THEY WILL HAVE TO STAND BEFORE YOUR JUDGMENT THRONE. THE NATIONS ARE ANGRY BECAUSE YOU GIVE REWARDS TO YOUR SAINTS AND THOSE WHO FEAR YOUR NAME. THE NATIONS ARE ANGRY BECAUSE YOU ARE DESTROYING THOSE WHO DESTROY THE EARTH AND HIS PEOPLE."

The angry voices of the damned did not reach Heaven. The open heart of God was now closed to them. Their blasphemies only echoed back to their ears. As they cursed God, they were only reminding themselves why they were lost. In His mercy, God did not allow His children in Heaven to again be vilified by the self-justifying curses of those left on earth. The peaceful silence of Heaven was interrupted only with the intermittent voices of praise to God.

In the meantime, the Tribulation scenes on earth were almost too horrible for John's tired eyes. But to be true to his commission, the Seer, faithfully observed this horrible and devastating time and recorded what he saw.

"I thank You that one day I will be with Jesus in Heaven," was John's responsive prayer. "Thank You for forgiving my sin." Once again, John worshiped God, "I worship You for Your protection of me all these years. Thank You that I still have life to serve You."

## Your Time to Worship

Lord, You created a perfect earth and said, "It is good," but satan brought disorder and corruption. I praise You that one day You will restore order and righteousness to this world.

Lord, You have given every person a chance to choose Your rule, but many still reject You. I praise You for allowing me to choose You and follow You.

Lord, the unsaved world does not know when payday will come. Because they continue to commit sins and crimes without suffering consequences, they think they've escaped judgment in hell. But one day, You will judge them. I thank You that Christ took my judgment.

Lord, those who deny You in life, also reject You in judgment. Thank You for accepting me in life and protecting me against condemnation.

Lord, all the "pleasures" that now tempt us, will one day be gone. Thank You for victory over sin this day and for separation from sin in eternity.

John's head was bowed in worship, when all of a sudden, his concentration was broken by the announcement of an angel...

"LOOK QUICKLY." John lifted his head. The angel explained, "LOOK NOW, BECAUSE YOU WILL SEE SOMETHING THAT HAS NEVER BEEN SEEN BY HUMAN EYES."

John now gazed at the Temple of God in Heaven. The incomparable beauty of this structure reminded him of the grandeur of Herod's temple on earth. But the inconceivable had happened more than 20 years earlier in

A.D. 70 No one had thought that the temple of Jerusalem could ever be destroyed, but the Roman General Titus had totally decimated the imposing work of architecture because Jewish zealots were using it as a fortress.

As a boy, John had always been overwhelmed when he saw the splendor of Herod's temple with its gold covered walls. However, as much as he had loved the temple, he was not grieved when the Roman soldiers desecrated it by offering a sacrifice to Zeus on its altars and tearing it apart stone by stone. Just as Jesus had predicted, the Romans had not left one stone upon another while searching for the melted gold that ran between the stones after the fires.

To John, the temple simply represented the old covenant where animals were sacrificed for sins. The death of Jesus had replaced the old covenant with a new age—the Church Age. So when the Romans destroyed Herod's temple, they actually eradicated any earthly remembrance that might attract Christians away from Christ.

Wrapped up in the darkness of the cave, John gazed into the city of light and stared at the Temple in the center of the city, as bright as a sun-filled day. John imagined how the original Solomon's temple might have appeared, yet he knew that the Temple splendor he saw in Heaven had to be more beautiful than the original temple built by Solomon.

Then John remembered that the voice had promised to show him something new...

*This Temple is not new to me,* John reflected. Although he had not seen this exact Temple before, he had seen one like it. *I've seen a temple many times,* he continued to reason within himself. *This is not new.*

John continued to wonder if this Temple he saw was new because it included a different pattern for the sanctuaries of God on earth. He knew Herod's temple and Solomon's temple and even before that—the tabernacle—all followed the same layout or design. God had originally given the blueprint for His sanctuary to Moses as he prayed on Mount Sinai in the wilderness.

Continuing to ponder this sight, John prayed...

Worship: When We First See the Ark, and The Seven Personages of the Future Tribulation

"Am I seeing the pattern for God's house on earth?"

As John continued to question why the voice had called this Temple some-thing new, all of a sudden, the veil that had been hiding from sight the Holy of Holies slowly began to open.

"I can see inside," John whispered nervously. "No one has ever been able to see into the Holy of Holies." This was the "thing that had never been seen by human eyes." Now, John—along with all those in Heaven—could see inside the Holy of Holies.

"This is amazing," John gasped out loud. "I'm looking into God's heart!"

True, the death of Jesus on the cross had made it possible for outsiders to look into the Holy of Holies. When Jesus had died, the curtain, which veiled the Holy of Holies from outsiders, had split from top to bottom. John smiled when he remembered that curtain—approximately 18 feet thick. While it was impossible for human hands to tear the massive cur-tain, the mighty hands of God had ripped it in half as a man might tear a leaf. Then John smiled again. The Jews had claimed that the earthquake had ripped the curtain, and subsequently, they quickly replaced the torn veil with a new one. Man had attempted to hide what God had opened.

But the Temple in Heaven was being opened so that John could see into the Holy of Holies. Like a breeze rushing into a vacuum, the unseeable was now seen. John's eyes rushed quickly back and forth to make sure he did not miss a thing. But there was only one article standing within the Holy of Holies.

John said, "I see the Ark of the Covenant."

Instinctively, shielding his eyes with his arms, John repeated the response of every believer when seeing the majesty of God—"Amen." John again fell on his face, for the Ark was the one place in the Old Testament where God had touched the earth. It was the one place in the Old Testament where the presence of God had manifested Himself when communicating with His people. John remembered what God had told Moses.

*I will meet with you, and I will speak with you from above the mercy seat, from between the two cherubim which are on the ark of the Testimony* [Covenant]... (Exodus 25:22).

John was sure that the Ark he saw in Heaven was not the actual Ark carried by Israel in the wilderness. Just as the Temple in Heaven was probably a pattern of God's house on earth, so the Ark he was seeing was a pattern of the one built in the wilderness.

John remembered all the rumors about the Ark of the Covenant. Some thought when Nebuchadnezzar had destroyed the temple in A.D. 586, the Ark had been buried in a secret cavern under the temple—in the Dome of the Rock—under the Holy of Holies. Others thought Nebuchadnezzar had given the Ark to Jeremiah the prophet, who buried it on Mt. Nebo, or on a Judean hill; or Jeremiah had taken it to Egypt for the renegade temple the Jews built at Tapaneese, on an island in the Nile delta. But wherever the Ark was, John was now looking into the Temple of Heaven, and he was seeing the real Ark of the Covenant.

### Your Time to Worship

Lord, I come to Your presence because there is no place else to go. I worship You.

Lord, even though I can't see You with my eyes, I can know You in my heart. I adore You.

Lord, even though You are everywhere present all the time, I want to get as close to You as I can. I want to be in Your heart because I need You.

Lord, You are so much greater than my experience, but I want to feel You as real as any person can. I want to touch You and have You touch me.

Lord, my emotions are so limited, and You are an unlimited God; but I want You to know, I love You.

While looking at the Ark, John felt closer to God than he had ever been before. For the Ark was the place where God dwelt with His people; it was the place God touched man. In the Ark (meaning, "box") were the two stone tablets where Moses had chiseled the Ten Commandments. The Ten Commandments given by God explained how He wanted His people to live. Also in the Ark was a symbolic pot of manna to remind God's people of His loving provision of food. When they had faced starvation, God continually fed them with manna. Finally, Aaron's rod that budded was in the box. When many rebelled against Moses as God's leader, God caused Aaron's rod (a dead stick) to blossom. This act reminded them that God can bring life out of death.

John, from his Patmos cave, continued to look into the Temple and gaze into the Holy of Holies. Then, he became aware that he was not the only one afforded this privilege. He turned his eyes away from the Temple to notice millions upon millions of observers in Heaven. They too were seeing what had never been seen before. All those in Heaven were gazing at the Ark of the Covenant with their actual eyes, and all other believers not yet in Heaven would see it through John's eyes; for the aged apostle would write it down so that future children of God could see into the Holy of Holies when they read the Book of Revelation.

As John gazed at the Ark of the Covenant, lightnings flashed and thunder rumbled down the hallways of Heaven, bouncing off the walls, then rolling towards the outer limits of space; just as lightnings and thunders had surrounded Mt. Sinai when God had met Moses there. Eventually, the pounding reverberations of thunder diminished until they were heard no longer.

All of Heaven worshiped God, for they were closer to seeing God than at any time before. Now, with their eyes, they were as close to God as they had been with their hearts when they had invited Jesus into their lives.

The four Seraphim guarding the throne, worshiped God on their faces. Immediately, the 24 saints followed their example, and next, the multitude of Heaven worshiped God as one person—millions times a million. All of Heaven bowed silently before God—as a servant waiting for a word from his master. All Heaven waited before God with their faces to the floor.

The silence of millions of worshipers times a million was overwhelming.

SILENCE!

How could anyone violate this sacred moment? John felt the weighty importance of the moment—millions upon millions of worshipers... still...quiet...waiting...a holy hush. The Temple of Heaven was reverent. Not knowing what to do or say, they waited for their Lord to give them direction. Likewise, John joined them from his cave. He too waited for God to speak.

## What I Learned From Seeing the Ark

I will enjoy things in Heaven that I can't even imagine while living on earth.

I will see things and learn things in Heaven that are hidden on earth.

I should expect phenomenal expressions from God when He reveals Himself.

I should expect the unsaved to be angry when God punishes them for their sin and rebellion.

I realize that just because God doesn't immediately judge sin in this life, it doesn't mean He will allow people to continually get away with rebelling against Him. There is judgment in the future.

## Section Six

### Scripture: Revelation 11:15–13:18

Lord, when the seventh angel blew his trumpet,
  You brought all people into Your presence
  Where they saw the original Temple in Heaven.
There was shouting, telling Heaven and earth,
  "The Kingdoms of this world
Have become the Kingdoms of Christ,
  And He will reign forever and ever."
The 24 saints bowed in worship to You,
  Prostrating themselves on the ground,
Saying, "We give thanks to You, the Almighty Lord God,
  You who are,
  You who were,
  And You who will always exist,"
Because You have exercised Your omnipotent power,
  And have begun to reign on the earth.
When You judged the nations, they were angry
  Because You judged them in wrath;
  They were not remorseful or repentant.
Now is the time to punish the wicked
  And reward Your servants and Your prophets,
  And those small and great who revered Your name,
Because You destroyed those who destroyed
  The earth and Your followers.

Lord, then the Temple in Heaven began to open for all to see,
  And behind the veil everyone could see clearly,
  All saw the Ark of the Covenant.
Suddenly, there were flashes of lightning,

Rumbling thunder, an earthquake,
And violent hail on earth.

## Seven Personages

Revelation chapters 12 and 13 depict seven personages (not called people because some of the individuals represent a group of people). These are seven personages that trace the history of satan's opposition to God's plan through Israel.

1. **Israel** — The women dressed in the sun is the nation Israel; the 12 stars are the 12 tribes of Israel; and the Man-Child is the Messiah-Deliverer (see Rev. 12:1). Throughout the Old Testament, satan tried to prevent the birth of the Messiah—Jesus Christ.

2. **Satan** — The red dragon is satan who uses earthly nations (crowns) to oppose Israel (see Rev. 12:3-4,9).

3. **Jesus** — The Man-Child is Jesus who will rule the world in the coming one thousand years of peace (see Rev. 12:5).

4. **Michael** — He is the archangel who opposes all satan tries to do to Israel and Jesus Christ (see Rev. 12:7).

5. **Saved Jews during the Tribulation** — The remnant of the woman's seed, i.e., Israel. Satan persecutes Israel during the last half of the Tribulation, but Israel flees to the desert (Petra) for protection.

6. **Antichrist** — The beast out of the sea (see Rev. 13:1) is the antichrist, or the false messiah. He will imitate Christ. The antichrist is raised from the dead (see Rev. 12:3,12), and wants everyone to worship him, in opposition to Christ who wants everyone to worship Him.

7. **The False Prophet** — The beast out of the earth is the false prophet (see Rev. 13:11). He is the third person of the unholy triad. Satan wants to be like the Father (see Isa. 14:14); the antichrist takes the place of Jesus; and the false prophet imitates the works of the Holy Spirit. Just as the Holy Spirit exalts Jesus Christ (see John. 16:14), the false prophet tries to entice the world to worship the antichrist during the Tribulation.

*1. Israel*

Lord, then John saw a woman in Heaven clothed with the sun,
     With the moon beneath her feet.
  The woman was the nation Israel
     From whom God promised the Deliverer would come.
  Israel was constantly persecuted by satan,
     Because he wanted to prevent the Deliverer from being born.

*2. Satan*

Lord, John also saw satan as an enormous dragon,
     Controlling seven nation-rulers,
     With ten horns and a crown on each head.
  Satan pulled one third of the fallen angels
     With him when he was banished from Heaven to earth.

*3. Jesus*

Lord, satan tried to kill those in the line of the Deliverer
     So He wouldn't be born;
     Satan knew the Messiah would one day rule over the earth.
  The Deliverer-Jesus completed Your work on earth,
     And You received Him back into Heaven.

## 4. Michael the Archangel

> There was war in Heaven where Michael the Archangel
>> Fought against the devil and his fallen angels.
> Satan was cast out of Heaven to earth
>> To complete his evil desire on earth.
> Satan is also called the devil, the serpent,
>> Who tries to lead the whole world into sin.

> Lord, You shouted with a loud voice,
>> "Victory, and power, and rulership
>> Now belong to Me."
> You shouted, "Now Jesus Christ can rule; satan is cast down;
>> He will no longer persecute Christians;
>> He will no longer accuse the brethren to Me."

> Satan is beaten by the blood of the Lamb
>> And by the faithfulness of martyrs
>> Who did not hold onto life in the face of death.
> You said, "Let Heaven and its citizens rejoice,
>> But to those on earth beware."
> Satan is angrily coming to persecute believers,
>> Because he knows his time is short.
> When satan found himself cast to the earth,
>> He turned his anger against the Jews,
>> Because Jesus the Messiah came from them.

## 5. The Remnant of Israel

> During the last half of the Tribulation,
>> Israel escaped to the wilderness,
>> Away from the devil who persecuted her.
> Israel stayed in the desert fortress of Petra
>> For three and a half years,
>> During the last half of the Tribulation.
> Every scheme of satan to destroy Israel

Was thwarted by the desert.
Then satan determined to punish every
Follower of Christ left on the earth.

## 6. The Antichrist

Lord, John saw a terrible animal emerge from the sea.
It was the antichrist, the false messiah.
The antichrist had in his hand seven nation-rulers,
And the antichrist had crowns on his ten horns.
He controlled the ten nations of the revived Roman Empire.
The antichrist was opportunistically like a leopard,
But ferocious like a bear,
And wanted to rule like the king of the jungle—the lion.
Satan gave the antichrist the same power he possessed,
And allowed the antichrist to rule the world for him.
One of the antichrist's seven heads had been killed,
But the antichrist came back to life,
So that multitudes marveled and followed him.
The antichrist, in a very persuasive speech, blasphemed You,
And slandered Your Temple and those who follow You.
Satan gave the antichrist power to fight against Your people,
To overcome them for three and a half years,
And to rule every ethnic group, language, and nation.
Everyone worshiped the antichrist except those
Whose names were in the Lamb's Book of Life,
And those who the antichrist had killed.

Lord, You said, "Those who have ears
To hear spiritual messages,
Listen carefully to what will happen."
Christians will be arrested, taken away, and imprisoned;
Other believers will be killed.
This will be an opportunity for Your children
To demonstrate their endurance and faith.

## 7. *The False Prophet*

Lord, John saw another terrible animal emerge from the sea
        Who tried to look like a lamb,
        But he had a haunting voice like satan.
    The second animal—the false prophet—served the antichrist,
        And propagated his influence everywhere.
    He pointed out the antichrist's fatal wound and told everyone
        How he had been raised from the dead,
        Persuading everyone to worship the antichrist.
    The antichrist organized his own "church"
        Bringing down fire from Heaven,
        Just as You sent fire on Pentecost.
    The false prophet did miracles to convince everyone
        To follow the antichrist.
    The false prophet erected a statue (idol) to the antichrist,
        Showing the wound that killed him,
        Yet also showing that the antichrist was now alive.
    The false prophet breathed in the statue of the antichrist
        So that it spoke his word.
    Those who refused to worship the antichrist's statue
        Were put to death.
    The false prophet ordered everyone to be branded
        With the brand of the antichrist
        In their forehead or right hand.
    Everyone was branded no matter how young or old,
        Rich or poor, slave or citizen.
    And no one could buy or sell anything,
        Unless they were branded
        With the name of the antichrist or his number.
    Anyone can calculate the number of the antichrist—
        It is 666.
        Amen.

# Section Seven

# The Unknown Song of the 144,000

## Scripture: Revelation 14:1-20

The Sunday sun was falling in the west, the dark fingers of afternoon shadows stretched across the backs of the kneeling worshipers in front of John's cave. The threat of the morning storms had evaporated. Praying deep within the belly of the mountain, the aged apostle had been absorbed by visions for hours, and because the setting sunrays couldn't reach him, he didn't realize the time of day.

John should have been getting tired...after all, he was over 90 years old. But the presence of God invigorated him. He was driven by passion.

Soon, another vision appeared to him. Just as his watery eyes had gazed upon Jesus earlier in the day, so now he saw Him standing in the center of Heaven—standing on Mount Zion...the Eternal City...Jerusalem.

John's heart missed a beat. Mount Zion, called the Upper City of Jerusalem, held many warm memories—he knew every street blindfolded. His father, Zebedee, had made enough money while fishing to purchase a home on Mount Zion, and young John ran through its streets as a teenager. Now in a vision, the aged John was revisiting the beloved city of his adolescence.

The rock covered streets and white plastered homes were as real as John remembered them, except he couldn't touch their tall white walls with his hands, nor could his feet walk its dusty streets. He simply visited with his eyes.

In his vision, Jesus was walking on Mount Zion, just as He had walked there toward the upper room on the evening of the Last Supper. The Master knew His way around Mount Zion, just as John did.

There was also a great multitude with Jesus who were all dressed in white—not the everyday white tunics, but in a pure white linen…a spotless white…the dress of the martyrs. John's ears, while failing, could now hear the shout…

"THESE ARE MADE CLEAN BY THE BLOOD OF THE LAMB."

These martyrs seemed to be the same ones he had seen earlier. John's memory was foggy—he wasn't sure. He knew he had previously seen martyrs; he recognized them by their clothing. He knew the those martyrs had come out of the Great Tribulation, but had these martyrs died at different times than the previous ones? John's mind was playing tricks with him—they did look the same.

He then saw the name of the Father branded on the martyrs' foreheads. They had identified with the Father, even to the point of death. But, on the other hand, what about those who had refused the identity of the Father? The number 666 had been engraved in the forehead and hands of the unsaved who lived during the Tribulation. They had submitted themselves to satan in order to buy food, clothes, and anything else.

Seeing the courage of these martyrs bolstered John's faith.

They had made a life-changing decision to follow Jesus. In their conversion experience, they had turned their back on the world's system and sin's temptation. Trusting God had been more than a single event to them; daily, they had recommitted their life to Christ. Every time they had tried to purchase food, they were refused because they had decided to follow Jesus. Without the 666 insignia, their money was useless. So daily, their choice was Jesus or food…Jesus or clothing…Jesus or necessities.

These martyrs had been given a choice—renounce Jesus or die! Somewhere along the line, they could have chosen to live, but that would have included a decision to reject Jesus. These martyrs with the Father's name on their forehead had chosen daily to follow Jesus to death.

A decision to die is contrary to the instincts of the flesh. The human nature yearns to live…as happy as possible…as pain-free as possible…as long as possible. When these martyrs had chosen the name of the Father rather than the number 666, they had chosen to suffer for Jesus. Because their Master had suffered for them on the cross, it was the least they could do.

John watched the martyrs following Jesus and was envious of their experience. Although he was suffering on Patmos, he considered his pain superficial. Their pain had been terminal. John knew he would not die a violent death. Jesus had said that Peter and the other disciples would die for their faith, but not John.

These martyrs whom John was watching gave new meaning to the phrase, "I die daily." Theirs was not just a death to evil impulse, nor was their death a crucifixion of the old nature. They had experienced hunger—a constant, gnawing pain slowly eating away at their life. Daily these martyrs lost strength, until death ended their ordeal. They could have ended their suffering simply by accepting the number 666 in their forehead, but instead, they chose the Father's name and with it, they chose martyrdom and received eternal life.

When John discovered that there were 144,000 standing at Mount Zion with Jesus, he knew they must be the martyrs he saw earlier for they were the same number as before.

"Thank You, Lord, for those willing to die for You," John worshiped from his cave. He paused in reverence for the martyrs. Those who had been burned in fire now stood in their new glorified bodies with Jesus...no smell of smoke, no trace of fire. Those who had been torn apart by wild beasts but now whole in body, stood with Jesus...no tears...no remorse. Those who had been starved, now appeared well fed...healthy...happy.

The martyrs did not pray for revenge upon their enemies; they were only interested in surrounding Jesus the Lamb, and their eyes were fixed on Him. Nothing in Heaven distracted them—not the angels, not the 24 saints, not the four angelic worship leaders around the throne. They had been martyred for the cause of Jesus; now they wanted to worship Him.

The next moment, John was distracted by a growing noise, sounding louder as it moved toward him. He turned to look further into the dark cave, but the sound was not coming from deep within the mountains, nor did it come from outside. The surging noise was coming from his vision. And it was becoming louder, as though he were standing next to a waterfall. Then the sound grew much louder than a waterfall; it bellowed like thunder bouncing across the hills. Yet it was not thunder, for it would eventually quiet as it rolled out of hearing. Instead, this sound grew progressively louder in John's ears. He was hearing the sound of the saved coming toward him.

What had been noise the previous moment now changed to the distinct sound of human voices. John heard voices singing—loud singing. On many occasions, John had heard people cheering so loudly he couldn't understand what they were saying. This time, he could hear human words, yet couldn't understand their meaning. It was not the yell of men fighting in battle; it was a happy sound…it was music…it was a gigantic singing choir.

John had heard the Levitical choirs in the temple many times, their precise trained voices giving glory to God. Because these choirs had been so accurately trained, John could understand every word they sang. And when the choirs in Jerusalem glorified God, John joined them in praise.

But John couldn't understand the triumphant words he now heard in the vision. He cupped his hands behind his ears, but to no avail. He still couldn't understand the music. Cocking his ear to the left…then to the right…he still couldn't understand.

The martyrs were singing new words to a new song John had never heard. They were singing to a new meter—the music was different. The Levitical choir had sung in a minor chord, but this was a new joyous song, completely foreign to John.

He hadn't heard music like this in the churches of Egypt, Cypress, Asia Minor, or Greece. Nor was it the music of the Romans. It was entirely new,…and John the apostle liked it. The new music made him want to praise God. However, he couldn't join them because he didn't know the words, nor did he know the tune. Somewhat perplexed, John began to ask some questions in prayer…

"What is this new song, and why can't I sing this song of praise with the 144,000?"

Anytime John had encountered people worshiping God, he wanted to join them. When he had visited the different churches with their different languages or dialects, and their different music, he had never felt strange or left out. Even when believers had worshiped God in a different language, John had joined them, singing in his own language. The language of the heart knows no boundaries. Worship from the heart crosses linguistic, ethnic, and class barriers. And just as John had worshiped with many language groups before, he now wanted to worship with the 144,000…but couldn't. The circumstances were different.

But the problem was not the distance between the cave on Patmos and Mount Zion in Heaven. God answered…

"THE 144,000 MARTYRS ARE SINGING A NEW SONG. NO ONE CAN KNOW THIS NEW SONG EXCEPT THOSE WHO HAVE DIED FOR ME."

God explained they were singing the martyrs' song. Only those who had tasted death—as Jesus had tasted death—could sing with them. Dying as a martyr had given them a unique experience, assuring their love for Jesus was 100 percent pure, and their commitment to Jesus was total. Many others in the Church had claimed to have totally loved Jesus, but there had been dark pockets of resistance in their hearts. They had held back from total devotion, yet the martyrs had held back nothing.

The new song was lovely to John's ears. The martyrs joyfully sang, unlike any human voices. Their singing sounded as beautiful as the music of a harp.

## Your Time to Worship

Lord, when I hear others worshiping You, I am grateful that You receive us all.

Lord, when I see others worshiping You, I identify with them and exalt You even higher.

Lord, when I find myself with others who are worshiping You, they motivate me to deeper expressions of my heart. I am grateful for corporate worship.

Lord, when I don't receive what others do, thank You for what I have. I praise You for who You are!

Lord, thank You that martyrs praise You; thank You for remembering them. May I live for You as they died for You.

John left the table where he had written the vision. Kneeling with his face to God on the cold stone floor, he worshiped the Lamb.

Although he couldn't worship with the new song of the martyrs, for only they knew the words, John worshiped God for protecting him from danger...for deliverance from physical suffering...for long life. A moment ago, John had been envious that he was not a martyr; now the old apostle was grateful for a peaceful life.

"Thank You for over 90 years of life," John offered his gratitude to God. Tears forced their way through his squeezed eyelids, and he thought, *What is harder—to die for Jesus...or to live for Jesus?*

The eleven disciples who had followed Jesus—John's friends—all had been martyred for their faith. Peter had been horribly crucified—upside down; Paul had been soaked with tar, then set aflame in Nero's garden to be slowly burned on a stake. Just as he had been a blazing witness for God in life, he likewise died in burning flames.

*Why have I been spared? Why haven't I died as a martyr?* John wondered and then thanked God for a life free from suffering.

John remembered the night before Jesus had died. It was at the Last Supper that Jesus had told His disciples they would desert Him. Even though barely 20 years old at the time, John remembered his youthful courage and pledge…

"Though everyone else runs away, I won't."

When the Roman soldiers had arrested Jesus, John had followed at a distance. And when Jesus had been taken to Caiphas' house for the religious trial, John had been downstairs in the courtyard. When the soldiers had hoisted the cross into the sky, John had watched in disbelief, not knowing what to do. He then remembered Jesus telling him from the cross…

"Son, behold your mother." Jesus gave him the care of Mary. Then to make sure there was no misunderstanding, Jesus told Mary, "Woman, behold your son."

Because John had followed all the way to the cross—facing the possibility of death—God had promised that he would die a natural death in old age. The other disciples who had run from death would eventually become martyrs. John knew their stories. When given a second chance, none of the other disciples had backed away, and all had died violent deaths for Jesus.

John bowed on the hard stone floor of the cave. He was no longer in a prophetic spirit; John was no longer seeing a vision. He was worshiping God, because although many Christians were suffering across the Roman world, their future was secure. After death, they would be with Jesus, worshiping Him. John was thankful for hope, and even from a cold cave, he worshiped Jesus. Shortly, he would return to his table where he would continue to write the vision—this time relaying how martyrs would worship in the future.

## What I Learned From the Lamb on Mount Zion

I can worship God because of the things I remember about Him from my recessive memory.

I need to faithfully reflect the Father's name, as martyrs in the past were faithful to proclaim His name.

I will receive a special message from God when I do special things for Him, as did the martyrs.

I will have a special place with God if I do not defile myself sexually, or any other way.

I must commit myself to follow the Lord without hesitation, as did the martyrs.

I realize that martyrs are closest to the heart of God, because they have given the most for the glory of God.

## Section Seven

### Scripture: Revelation 14:1-20

Lord, John saw the Lamb—Jesus standing on Mount Zion
      In the city of Jerusalem;
   With Him were 144,000 martyrs.
      They had Your name written on their foreheads.
John heard a growing sound
      Like a roar of a great waterfall,
      Like rolling thunder over the plains.
Yet the sound was pleasing, like the singing of a choir
      Accompanied by harps.
The martyrs were singing a new song
      In front of Your throne.
The four Seraphim were worshiping with them,
      So were the 24 saints on their thrones.
Only the 144,000 could learn the new hymn
      Because they had been redeemed
      From the suffering and tribulations of earth.
These had not defiled themselves spiritually;
      They were as pure as virgins.
Because they had followed the Lamb in persecution,
      They were redeemed from tribulation.
      They are a firstfruits offering to You.
They never told a lie,
      And their lives were blameless.

Lord, John saw an angel flying over Heaven,
      Announcing the end was near.
The Good News has been preached to all people—
      To every ethnic group, language, and nation on earth.

The angel shouted, "Fear God and praise Him,
  For His time has come to sit in judgment;
  Everyone worship the Creator of Heaven and earth."

Lord, John saw another angel shouting, "All people
  Who worshiped the antichrist,
    And branded themselves with his brand,
  Must drink the wine of judgment that is poured out
    By God who is angry against sin."
They will be tortured in the presence
  Of Your holy angels and the Lamb,
    And the smoke of their torture rises forever and ever.
There will be no relief for them day or night,
  Because they worshiped the beast and his statues,
    And accepted his branding in their right hand and foreheads.

Lord, John wrote, "Christians must remain faithful in persecution
  Because the antichrist will be judged,
    And the unsaved will be punished."
Then John was told to write, "Happy are those
  Who die in the Lord during the Tribulation."
The Holy Spirit said, "They will rest from their trials,
  Forever in the Lord,
    For their good works will follow them."
Again, John looked to see Jesus—the Son of Man,
  Sitting on a cloud
    With a golden crown on His head.
He had a sharp sickle in his hand
  Ready to go to work.
Another angel came out of the Temple and shouted
  To Jesus sitting on the cloud,
"The time has come; use the sickle on earth,
  For sin is ripe and ready to be harvested.
    The people of the earth have gathered to fight You."

Then He swung His sickle against all unsaved people,
> Gathering them for judgment before Your throne.
Another angel who also had a sickle
> Came out of the Temple to tell Jesus,
"Put Your sickle to work to cut all the grapes
> From the vine of the earth,
> Because sin is abundantly ripe."
So the sickle was put to the harvest,
> And filled the wine press of God's anger
> With the people of the earth.
It was the battle of the valley of Armageddon.
> And blood ran in a river 200 miles long,
> As high as a horse's bridle.
>> Amen.

# Section Eight

# WORSHIPING THE LAMB

**Scripture: Revelation 15:1–18:24**

John continued to sit at his crude table, writing down everything he saw in one prophetic vision after another. He had looked into Heaven to see one worship scene after another, each one separated by terrible pictures of judgment on earth. Like a gigantic parenthesis or reprieve, each beautiful vision of people worshiping God made it easier for John to write the next scenes of horrendous judgments. John bowed his head over the many pages of his manuscript and prayed...

"Lord, how much longer will You punish the earth?" The old apostle knew that God would have to cleanse the earth of every taint of sin. Again he asked, "How long?" He listened for the response, and then heard an answer...

"Shortly..."

John lifted his tired head to once more gaze into the vision. There in the center of Heaven, John saw seven angels—busy, preparing to do something, although John wasn't sure what they would do.

What John didn't immediately realize was that God was showing him these angels in answer to his question. These seven angels would pour out the final judgment of God on the earth. Then it would be over.

God had not shown John everything; indeed, Heaven was so large that it was impossible for John to see everything from his cave in Patmos. But God had yet to show something special to John—something he had not seen...

A beautiful, calm, glistening sea.

Without one ripple breaking upon its surface, the sea reflected a beautiful red glow, and John thought he was watching a dazzling sunset. The sea glowed as it if were on fire.

Then John saw a multitude standing on the red sea—not as large as the entire multitude in Heaven, nor as large as the 144,000. They were standing on the sea that glowed like fire, and they were singing.

*Who are these?* the Seer asked himself. He peered long, looking from face to face, trying to determine the answer.

A voice then interrupted John's thoughts and informed him, "These are the ones who were victorious in the Great Tribulation. They refused to bow down to the image of the antichrist or place idols in their homes." These people standing on the glowing red sea had taken a stand against the evil system of satan and had prevailed. They had not accepted the antichrist's number—666—in their hand or forehead and had refused to let satan control their lives. But this crowd had been victorious over satan, unlike the 144,000 martyrs who were killed when they also refused to submit to the antichrist.

*What are they singing?* John searched his failing memory for the name of the familiar hymn he heard. He could recall that it was a song that he had sung as a youth in the synagogue of Caperneum, but he couldn't remember its title. He listened to its familiar refrain, and then hummed the words. Suddenly, it came back to him, and he said aloud to no one in particular, "They are singing the song of Moses."

John remembered it was a hymn of victory. When Moses and Israel had triumphed over Pharaoh and Egypt, they had sung a psalm of triumph. They had won a religious battle between the gods of Egypt and the God of Israel. It had been a battle of two opposing wills—would Pharaoh rule God's people or would God rule His people? When Pharaoh's 600 chariots had been ready to attack Israel, God had blown the wind upon the Red Sea, pushing back its waters. Then the children of Israel had crossed over to the other side on dry ground. When Pharaoh had tried to follow Israel, God withdrew His wind that had been holding back the sea, and

116

all the Egyptians drowned along with Pharaoh. On the other side, Moses led Israel in singing…

*I will sing unto the Lord,*
        *For He has triumphed gloriously.*
*Pharaoh's horses and chariots threatened me;*
        *They were destroyed by the sea.*
*The Lord is my strength and song;*
        *He has become my salvation.*
*The Lord is a man of war;*
        *His name is the powerful Jehovah.*
*Pharaoh's army has drowned in the Red Sea;*
        *His officers sank to the bottom as stones.*
*The Lord's right hand was gloriously revealed;*
        *He dashed in pieces the enemy.*
*In an excellent way God overthrew the Egyptians;*
        *God's wrath burned them as stubble.*
*God's breath blew the waters apart,*
        *And Israel passed over on dry land.*
*The enemy chased Israel into the bottom of the sea;*
        *Their lust drove them to their death.*
*God stopped breathing so the waters flooded the enemy;*
        *They sank as lead to their destruction.*
*What God is like unto the Lord?*
        *He is glorious in holiness and powerful in miracles.*
*God will bring Israel into the Promised Land;*
        *God will dwell in the sanctuary among His people.*
*Sing unto the Lord for He has triumphed gloriously.*
        *The Lord shall reign forever and ever.*
                        (Exodus 15:1-18, author's translation).

The words came back to John. He joyfully sang the song of Moses along with those in Heaven. Just as God had given Moses a great victory over Pharaoh, so this multitude had won a great victory over satan and his forces during the Tribulation. And just as Moses and the multitude had sung a victory song, so those in Heaven praised God with the same song.

John bowed his head to thank God for victory. Although he was presently a captive, by faith he knew one day he would be free. Although God's people were now being tormented by Rome throughout the Mediterranean world, by faith, each victim would be victorious. In the black cave, John's feeble voice sang the victory song of Moses, and pure light flooded his soul. The damp cave sparkled, and praise vanquished despair.

## Your Time to Worship

Lord, You are greater than our greatest fear, more powerful than our mighty enemy. I praise You for victory in my life.

Lord, You are more beautiful than our beauty, and more brilliant than our light. I magnify You for knowledge to see and understand.

Lord, You are superior to our best, and more mighty than our strength. I am grateful for Your strength to overcome.

Lord, You are truer than our standard of truth; You are more profound than our wisdom. I worship you with my limited human understanding.

Lord, You are everything and I am nothing; I cannot compare You with anything, for You are above comparison. You are all in all.

John's eyelids became tired, and he dozed. Had the melody put him to sleep? Or did he sleep because the music had stopped? He was mentally alert for a man over 90 years old, but his active mind was imprisoned by a frail body. Even though he resisted, John needed rest—just a catnap—to keep going. His gray hair spread out over the table as he dozed. Suddenly, the silence startled his subconscious. His head popped up, and he gazed into the darkness..

As John rubbed sleep from his eyes, his ears picked up another melody— a different song. Then in prophetic vision, John again saw the multitude singing in Heaven. They were still standing on the sea that glowed as a red fire. This time they were singing a different song. The multitudes in Heaven were composing their own song of triumph and worship, just as Moses had celebrated and composed his psalm of victory.

> *Great and marvelous are Your works;*
> > *You are Lord God Almighty.*
> *Just and true are Your ways;*
> > *You are King of the saints.*
> *How can we not fear You?*
> > *Your name is glorious.*
> *All nations shall come to worship You.*
> > *You only are holy.*
> *You have finally judged the earth;*
> > *You are faithful to Your Word.*

As the multitudes praised God for the great victory given them, John again slipped from his table to his knees. It was difficult seeing people worship God without joining them. The praise music of one person often motivates another to join in worship to God.

As John was worshiping God, he sensed something else happening, and lifted his head to look about Heaven. The quietness captured his attention. He wondered what everyone seemed to be waiting for and noticed that they were looking at the Temple in the center of Heaven. Something was happening there. Then John saw movement.

The Temple was opening again. Previously, he had looked inside the Temple to see the Ark of the Covenant. As John anticipated the next event, he wondered what he would see this time. Slowly, the doors opened...

The four Seraphim that surrounded the throne, the ones who did the special work of God, held the bowls of the wrath of God located in the Temple. These bowls contained the final and most severe judgments that God would pour out on the earth. The Seraphim gave one bowl to each of the seven waiting angels.

"This is the final judgment of God," John was told. "When these seven angels deliver their punishments to earth, God will have finished purging the earth."

Even though John knew he couldn't see God, he quickly looked back into the Temple, hoping to find Him. But all that John could see in the Temple of God was His wrath—bowls of wrath to be poured out on the earth.

John had constantly preached to his flock, "God is love," yet he knew in his heart that there was another truth—"God is holy."

As the Lawmaker of the universe, God's passion is driven by His love—He is not willing for any to perish. But God is also ruled by His holiness—He cannot allow any infraction of His law to go unpunished. If God forgives the lawbreaker by an arbitrary decision, God is not faithful to His nature and He ceases to keep His promise to punish sin.

In life, John preached God is love; he invited all to salvation through repentance and faith, because Jesus died to forgive any law they had broken. But after life is over and people have been given their final opportunity to repent, God must punish those who break His law. John looked at the seven bowls of God's judgment, then silently asked, "When will God begin the final judgment?

"NOW," John was told. "Now, the seven angels will deliver God's final punishment to the earth.

John watched as the seven angels left Heaven to deliver their judgment. Only after they had left was the Temple filled with smoke from the glory of God; and John could no longer see anything in the Temple. He remembered that God spoke out of thick darkness on Mount Sinai to Moses. He remembered that when God gave Moses the Ten Commandments on Sinai that the mountain peak was covered with dark clouds and lightnings. The same things were happening here. Now John understood why the clouds concealed the glory of God. God had revealed Himself in love, but covered His glory with thick clouds to preserve from judgment those who were observing the scene.

As much as John didn't want to describe more judgments in his book, he remained faithful to the commission given him by God. He continued to write how each of the seven angels poured out their bowls of judgment, resulting in death, suffering, and misery.

John carefully observed each angel and dutifully wrote what he saw and what each angel did. Finally, when the seventh angel delivered the last judgment, John heard a loud voice out of the Temple—the Temple filled with clouds—a voice that cried with anguish...

"IT IS FINISHED."

These had been the same words that Jesus had announced from the cross. When Jesus had finished dying for the sins of the world, He had claimed His victory from the cross with the words, "IT IS FINISHED." Over the years, John had wondered exactly what Jesus had meant. John had known that the physical life of Jesus was finished; but had there been a deeper meaning? Had Jesus meant, "The penalty against the sins of the world is finished"? Or perhaps Jesus had meant, "The animal sacrifices are finished." Because Jesus had introduced the "age of grace," perhaps he meant "The law as a way of life is finished."

Now 60 years later, John was hearing the same words again. He wondered what the phrase, "IT IS FINISHED" meant. John knew the last angel was pouring out the final judgment. But did it mean more? Did it mean, "The purification of earth is finished"; or did it mean, "The final wrath of God against rebellion is satisfied"?

As soon as John heard the words, "IT IS FINISHED," there appeared lightnings and thunder unlike he ever heard before. And the earth rumbled with a final earthquake, more mighty than before. If there were any thought that a vestige of civilization remained, this earthquake removed all doubt. God had once told Adam to subdue and have dominion over the earth—now everything accomplished by the sons of Adam in every age had been destroyed.

The earth was now prepared to return to its paradise.

## Your Time to Worship

Lord, I praise You because You bring everything to completion. You pronounced, "It is finished" over my salvation.

Lord, I thank You for completing Your plan in my life, writing, "It is finished" over Your guidance and protection.

Lord, I adore You because one day You will finish Your plan for this earth.

Lord, I worship You because one day You will complete the purpose for which You saved me. You will deliver me to Heaven, and You will make me perfect in Your presence.

John, ever the apostle of love, had looked upon the earth for any sign of worldwide repentance or massive turning to God. There had been none. In its place, men had continued to blaspheme God for His judgment on the earth. To the end, John had searched for people to respond to the love of God. But no! To the last opportunity, they had rebelled against Him even as He loved them. And when the end came, those who had been rebellious in life were rebellious in death.

## What I Learned From the Victor's Song

I can worship God with triumphant songs when God gives me victory over difficulties and persecution.

I can effectively worship God because of my experience, whether I am a martyr or whether I am victorious.

I can effectively worship God, singing songs written by others, or singing words from my own heart.

I will never fully know God because I am finite. (God is hidden by smoke and thick darkness.)

I should praise God for His goodness to us and for His punishment of sin.

I should praise God because His judgment of this earth will come to an end—"It is finished."

## Section Eight

### Scripture: Revelation 15:1–18:24

Lord, John then saw a sea without a ripple on its surface.
>The sea had glowing fire in the water.

Standing by the sea were those saints
>Who had triumphed against the antichrist.

They had refused to worship his statue;
>They had not been branded with the number 666.

They had harps and were singing
>The victorious song of Moses—
>How he defeated the Egyptians.

They also sang the song of the Lamb—Jesus,
>Who had given them victory over the antichrist.

"Great and wonderful is everything You do,
>Lord God Almighty.

Just and true are all Your ways.
>You are the King of the nations.

Who would not reverence and praise Your name,
>For you alone are holy?

All nations will come before You,
>To worship and adore You,
>For the righteous things You've done."

Lord, John saw another awful scene in Heaven.
>An angel was distributing the last seven judgments—
>Last, because they were to exhaust God's anger to sin.

John saw the temple of God opening,
>And he could look into the Holy of Holies.

Out came seven angels each with
>A different judgment from God.

Each angel had a pure white linen robe
    And a golden sash around his waist.
One of the Seraphim around the throne gave the seven angels
    Seven bowls filled with the anger of God.
Smoke from the glory of God filled the Temple,
    So that no one could enter
    Until the seven bowls of judgment were finished.

Lord, John heard a voice shout from the Temple to the seven angels,
    "Go pour Your seven bowls out over the earth."

*The First Bowl*

The first angel poured his bowl on the earth,
    And ugly painful sores broke out on all people
    Who had the brand 666 and worshiped the antichrist statue.

*The Second Bowl*

The second angel emptied his bowl on the oceans,
    And they turned to blood;
    Every living thing in them died.

*The Third Bowl*

The third angel poured his bowl into the rivers and springs.
    They also turned to blood.
Then the angel said, "Lord, You live now,
    And You lived in the past.
    You are Holy in Your judgments.
Because evil people have shed the blood of Your saints,
    So You have given them blood to drink.
    This is what they deserve."
The angel at the altar responded, "Yes, Lord, God Almighty,
    Your punishments are true and just."

*The Fourth Bowl*

> The fourth angel emptied his bowl on the sun,
>> So the sun scorched people
>> As if they were burned with fire.
> People cursed You for sending these judgments
>> Because they were severely burned by the sun,
>> But they would not repent and turn to You.

*The Fifth Bowl*

> The fifth angel emptied his bowl over
>> The throne of the antichrist,
>> And his empire was plunged into darkness.
> People bit their tongues in pain.
>> They continued to curse You,
>> And they refused to repent of their evil.

*The Sixth Bowl*

> The sixth angel emptied his bowl over the Euphrates River,
>> And all the water dried up.
> And the armies of the East crossed the dry river bed,
>> Heading to invade the Promised Land.
> Then came a message from the mouth of satan,
>> And the antichrist, and the false prophet,
> "To all the kings of the nations of the world,
>> Join us in fighting God Almighty.
> We will finally do away with the Jews
>> And fight the God of the Jews."
> Three foul spirits came out of their mouth like frogs;
>> They were demons sent to deliver the message
>> And convince the kings to wage war.
> All the armies of the world came to fight God
>> At the battle of Armageddon.
> Then God attacked them unexpectedly,

Like a thief in the night catches victims
When they do not expect violence.

## The Seventh Bowl

The seventh angel emptied his bowl into the air,
    And a voice shouted, "The end has come";
        For the last bowl was the sacred coming of Christ.
Then there were flashes of lightning, rolling thunder,
    And a violent earthquake that shook the earth,
        More violently than ever before.
The city of Jerusalem was split into three parts.
    The cities of the earth crumbled to earth.
The city of Babylon was not forgotten;
    It was punished with the violence of its crimes.
The islands of the ocean disappeared;
    No mountain was left standing.
Storms of hail weighing 100 pounds each fell from the sky.
    And the more fierce the punishment from God,
        The more people rebelled and cursed God.

## The Fall of Religious Babylon

Then one of the seven angels with bowls spoke to John,
    "Come, I will show you the punishment
        For the prostituted church of the antichrist."
The kings of the earth have committed sexual sins,
    By worshiping in his vile temple.
They have made the whole world sin against God
    By forcing them to partake of her adultery.
John was taken in the Spirit to see the prostitute,
    Riding on a scarlet red animal.
It had seven heads who were ruling leaders,
    And ten horns representing the revived Roman Empire.
        Blasphemy was written all over her.

The prostitute was dressed in purple and red
    With gaudy jewelry of gold and pearls.
She was drinking a cup of disgusting filthy fornication.
    On her forehead was written,
    "Babylon the Great, mother of all prostitutes."
The prostitute was drunken with the blood of martyrs
    Whom she had killed.
John stared at the prostitute in alarm.
    The angel said, "Don't be horrified.
    I will explain who the prostitute is and the beast she rides.
She is the pseudo-church of the antichrist which was alive,
    But she died and will come from the bottomless pit
    To eventually be destroyed.
Those whose names are in the Lamb's Book of Life
    Will be dumbfounded by this reappearance.
The seven heads represent seven rulers
    Who live in a city with seven hills.
Five leaders have already fallen, a sixth now reigns;
    The seventh is yet to come.
The scarlet red animal is the eighth ruler;
    He will come up from hell
    But will be destroyed and return there.
The ten horns are ten kings who don't yet have power;
    They will rule in the future for a short time,
    Providing their strength and authority for the antichrist's use.
They will war against the Lamb at Armageddon.
    But the Lamb is the Lord of lords and King of kings;
    He will defeat them and their followers."

The angel continued his explanation, "The waters
    Beside the prostitute are all the people who follow
    The antichrist from every people group, language,
    and nation.
But the ten rulers and the antichrist will turn against

The pseudo-church, stripping it of its rituals and power.
God will influence the minds of sinful people
To do His pleasure with the pseudo-church,
Until He comes to judge the antichrist and his followers."

## The Fall of Commercial Babylon

John saw another angel come from Heaven;
His brightness shined to all the earth.
He shouted, "Babylon is fallen, Babylon is fallen,
Which is the den of demons.
Every filthy spirit and every detestable idea
Also lives there.
All the nations have been intoxicated with
Her proposition to sin.
All the world leaders have committed adultery
With her and grown rich from her extravagance."
Then John heard a voice from Heaven,
"Come out from her, people of God.
Do not share in her crimes and sins.
God in Heaven knows about her sins.
She will be treated as she treated others;
She will be paid back double what punishment she gave out.
Every one of her sinful pleasures and luxuries
Will give her grief and misery.
She boasts that she is a queen on a throne;
She is not sorry for anything she's done.
Judgment will fall on her in a single day;
She'll suffer disease, mourning, and hunger.
You, Lord God, who has great power
Will burn her up.
The world rulers, who have fornicated with her,
Will weep and mourn for they lose everything.
When they see the smoke of commercial Babylon burning,

They will stay away at a safe distance and cry,
'Alas!...Alas! Our great city
    Babylon, a mighty city
    Was destroyed in a single hour.'
All the businesspeople of the earth will
    Weep and mourn over her,
Because no one will any longer buy
    Gold, silver, jewels, pearls, fine cloths,
    Perfumes, costly furniture, and sculptures.
They also cry for lack of oil, flour, wheat,
    Meat, and automobiles.
And no one will work anywhere because
    There is no money to pay anyone
    To do anything.
The expensive things they loved are gone, never to return.
    All the ease and pleasure have ceased.
The businesspeople who made a fortune out of
    Commercial Babylon will stand at a safe distance
    To wring their hands and grieve saying,
'This is terrible; what am I going to do?'
    Everything that was beautiful and fine
    And comfortable was destroyed in a single hour.
All the fashionable clothes, accumulated wealth,
    Exquisite meals, entertainment, and vacations
    Were all destroyed in a single hour.
All the captains of ships and people who
    Made a living from the sea,
    Stayed at a safe distance,
Watching the smoke as commercial Babylon burned, crying,
    'There has never been a civilization like this;
    We will never see anything like this again.
That great city—commercial Babylon—that kept

Us rich through her excesses,
Was ruined in a single hour.'"

Yet, there was rejoicing in Heaven, from all
The saints, apostles, and prophets;
For You judged an economic system that persecuted them.
You judged a way of life that rebelled against righteousness.

Then a mighty angel lifted a huge mill-stone
And threw it into the ocean saying,
"So shall this commercial way of life
Never be heard from again.
Never again will there be the sound of music,
Dancing, reverie, and the laughter of pleasure seekers.
Never again will there be the sound of machines in factories
Or the ring of cash registers, or any business ventures.
There will be no electricity; everything will be dark.
Every machine that runs will shut down.
There'll be no laughing like people in love,
And no one will achieve their heart's desire.
All your luxuries, entertainment, and pleasures
Will be gone forever;
For in commercial Babylon is found the blood of martyrs
Who were destroyed by her way of life."
Amen.

# Section Nine

## WORSHIP AT THE
## MARRIAGE SUPPER OF THE LAMB

### Scripture: Revelation chapters 19–20

John's tired eyes were closed. His face was bowed to the ground in worship to God—it was his only response to the last vision he had seen. He had not looked up for quite awhile. The Seer was having difficulty coming to terms with the atrocities that had been shown in his vision at the end of the Tribulation. It seemed like the wrath intensified as the end approach.

John believed in God, but he had difficulty understanding the extent of the devastation that unfolded before him. While John had not left his cave, nor had he grown any older, even so he had just experienced seven years—seven horrible years of Tribulation wrath poured out on the earth.

John saw the carnage of war with its ensuing starvation, homelessness, and inflation. He saw the pale horse bringing death to 25 percent of the world. He saw persecution spread to God's servants—ultimately 144,000 were martyred.

Next, John saw lightning plummeting to the earth, burning almost a third of the forests in flames. Giant hail stones killed people in the open fields. Then, John witnessed a meteoric fireball plunging into the ocean, claiming approximately a third of all life in the sea. The stability of the universe came unglued, comets plunged to the earth, poison from the sky contaminated much of the drinking water. Earthquakes rumbled across the continents, creating more fires and blinding smoke that blanketed the sun, blocking out its life-giving rays. Disease and sickness spread unchecked.

John shut his eyes to the destruction caused by a herd of demonic spirits spreading out over the earth to do the work of satan and the antichrist.

With the stench of death everywhere, John wearily asked, "Is that all?" But God was not finished with judgment until every wrong had been righted and every transgression punished. Poison in the atmosphere continued to produce grievous sores; rotting corpses of sea creatures in the ocean produced nauseous fumes. A foul stench turned the stomachs of even the strongest men. With no pure water to quench their thirst, and toxic poisons in the sky burning up the ozone layer, the scorching sun burned the bodies of those dying slowly from starvation and thirst.

With suffering everywhere, no one trusted another. Fathers turned against sons, and mothers against their families. Driven by excruciating thirst for fresh water and food to satisfy their hunger, the earth was filled with rioting and looting, and a once civilized people murdered one another over something as insignificant as a piece of bread.

When it seemed as though nothing worse could happen, the antichrist called for the nations to attack Israel in the Promised Land. They knew that in God's city—Jerusalem—the city of peace, people were smiling because of the blessings of God. There was water to drink and food to eat, and the city had not been influenced by the collapse of the corrupt monetary system of the world leader. None of those who were living under God's protection in Jerusalem had the mark of 666 upon their foreheads or hands.

Because of the peace of God's people, in contrast to the anger of those who hated God's people, the antichrist called the world to a final solution of the Jews. Consequently, they planned to march into the Holy Land, and once and for all slaughter all the Jews—a holocaust to solve the Jewish dilemma.

In the final moments of the Tribulation, God finally retaliated against the antichrist and his worldly system. He destroyed the prostitute Babylon, including all her wealth, beauty, and earthly desires—in one day. Those who saw it gasped; they couldn't believe that their magnificent Babylon could disappear so suddenly.

John saw the entire seven years of carnage through the power of prophetic vision. While it was horrible to witness, John realized it would all happen in the future as God predicted. In the coming seven years of Tribulation, the horror of its experience would be worse than any futuristic dream he saw.

Old John's knees creaked as he bowed in worship and prayer. Humility was a position that suited him. He thanked God again for salvation and for daily protection. He thanked God for the safety of the cold cave and for meager bread on the table waiting for him.

But even though John's spirit was comfortable bowing before God, his ancient knees began to rebel. As his heart sought to remain longer in the presence of God, his aching body needed rest.

## Your Time to Worship

Lord, I don't understand all You've done for me on the cross, but I thank You for salvation.

Lord, I don't see all You do for me each day, but I praise You for supernatural guidance and protection.

Lord, I don't know why You let me serve You, because I am so feeble compared to Your power; but I am grateful for the opportunity to be Your slave.

Lord, I don't know why You hear my prayers, because I am so limited and I don't know how to pray; but I continually lift up Your name in praise.

Lord, there's much about my faith I don't understand, but I know enough to worship You, and I know enough to trust my future to You.

Deep within the dark cave, John heard an approaching rumble coming from his vision of the endtimes. *Is there yet more?* he inwardly asked. *Does God have more earthquakes for the earth?* The old apostle tilted his ear to listen. At the same time, he looked with his prophetic eyes, waiting for God to show him another scene of the future. This time, however, God didn't show him a scene—just a sound. He lifted his bowed head, and his eyes peered through the darkness to see beyond the stone walls of the cave. Then John's eyes turned upward, looking toward Heaven...

Then he realized the sound was not an earthquake, nor was it the loud banging of crashing buildings. The sound was a word—a pronounced word, though John couldn't tell what was being said. At first he heard it softly, muted...

*That's it!*

It was a Jewish word, one that he had heard back home as a boy in the synagogue.

John remembered the word and smiled. He had first heard the word from the old rabbis in the synagogue reading the Psalms. Each time those godly fishermen from Capernaum would read the word, they stopped, then pronounced it distinctly. It was attached to no other word—it stood alone. When the old men read the word, all the worshipers in that white-stone synagogue would repeat the word in unison. And John now heard it spiraling down the cave toward him. It was not spoken by one, but by many, simultaneously, their voices like thunder rolling down a valley...bouncing off the mountainsides...growing louder....

"HALLELUJAH."

When the shout finally filled the cave, John repeated the Hebrew meaning to the word, "Praise the Lord." John laughed, nodding his head in approval, for he too was saying in his heart, "HALLELUJAH!" Then John heard a second antiphonal wave sweep down the cave filling the chamber, "HALLELUJAH." Then he heard angels singing...

"SALVATION...AND GLORY...AND HONOR...AND POWER... UNTO THE LORD, OUR GOD."

When the angels sang "SALVATION," John echoed in his heart, "Thank You for salvation...." When the angels sang "GLORY," John prayed, "Be glorified in my life...bring glory to Yourself...You have all power...." John knew that all people in Heaven were worshiping God because He had finished the judgment of seven years of tribulation on the earth. Just as the farmer knows that rain brings life, John knew that with the Tribulation and judgments, God was ushering in life and Heaven.

"HALLELUJAH!"

All Heaven worshiped God saying, "YOU HAVE DONE THE RIGHT THING. YOU HAVE BEEN TRUE TO YOUR PROMISES. YOU HAVE JUDGED BABYLON, THE GREAT PROSTITUTE WHO CORRUPTED THE EARTH WITH HER SIN."

"HALLELUJAH!"

God was worshiped, "YOU HAVE CLEANSED THE EARTH. YOU HAVE PREPARED IT FOR ETERNITY. HALLELUJAH!"

When John heard the voices of Heaven, he again nodded his head. The old man agreed with the people of Heaven that tribulation and judgment of sin had been necessary.

Then John realized that he was still on the Isle of Patmos as a prisoner, and there were thousands of other Christians in the Mediterranean world who remained imprisoned by the Roman Empire. Their tribulation was not over. John's response was to pray for his Roman guards, just as Jesus prayed for the Roman soldiers who had nailed Him to the cross...

*"Father, forgive them...."*

John prayed for the salvation of Roman oppressors everywhere. But if they wouldn't repent, what would God have to do? John knew the Father would one day judge all those who had persecuted Christians.

Again, John heard the voices deep within the cave echoing from Heaven, "HALLELUJAH...GOD HAS AVENGED THE MURDER OF

HIS SERVANTS." Tears filled John's eyes as he continued to thank God for His goodness.

A silence came across Heaven…a holy hush. John lifted his eyes to see the focus of Heaven on the throne and those who sat about Him. The four Seraphim worship leaders had lifted their hands to command silence. Then before them, the 24 living saints fell to their faces, worshiping God. They broke the silence with a shout,

"HALLELUJAH…"

The four angels at the four corners of the throne of God joined them shouting,

"HALLELUJAH."

Then one of the saints from 24 thrones spoke to the multitude…

"Bow down—worship God. All people—the young—the aged—everyone worship God."

Just when John thought nothing else could be added, he heard the great crowd of Heaven erupt into another worship theme, like a multitude of ocean waves breaking upon the rocks at one time. He heard the crashing sound…

"HALLELUJAH FOR THE LORD GOD ALMIGHTY REIGNS."

John felt in his bones that something terminal was about to happen in Heaven. Even though the old apostle was a stranger to the throne room of God, he felt something awesome was to occur. Not only John, but the 24 saints and the four Seraphim anticipated it as well. The vast multitudes held their breath. All were hoping for something, but didn't know what to expect. Then with a gigantic voice that reached all of Heaven, a great angel announced…

"REJOICE AND WORSHIP GOD BECAUSE THE TIME IS COME FOR THE WEDDING FEAST OF THE LAMB OF GOD. THE BRIDE WILL BE THOSE BLOOD-BOUGHT BELIEVERS WHO HAVE CLOTHED THEMSELVES IN THE FINEST WHITE LINEN ROBES,

WHICH REPRESENT THE RIGHTEOUS DEEDS DONE BY THE PEOPLE OF GOD."

## Your Time to Worship

Because Your power from the beginning stretches into eternity, I shout "Hallelujah" for Your present Almighty protection on me.

Because Your perfect wisdom is evident from past creation stretching into the future Heaven, I shout "Hallelujah" for Your wise plan for my life right now.

Because Your accurate judgment punishes only those who should be punished, I shout "Hallelujah" for Your faithfulness to keep Your promise of judgment and reward.

Because Your presence is everywhere in this world to help and keep me, I shout "Hallelujah" for Your love and care for me.

Because of Your unswerving promise to return to receive me to Yourself, I shout "Hallelujah."

The angel whose voice had been heard, once again made the announcement that echoed throughout the throne room, down the aisles of the great crowd, and out into eternity...

"BLESSED ARE THOSE WHO ARE INVITED TO THE WEDDING FEAST OF THE LAMB."

When John heard the great invitation, he knew that the time of the end had finally come. He remembered the parable that Jesus had told about ten virgins preparing themselves for the wedding feast. There were five wise bridesmaids and five foolish bridesmaids. John remembered that the five foolish virgins didn't have oil for their lamps, and when the time of the end came, they were shut out.

John knew this was the time for the wedding feast to begin. Christ would fully manifest Himself to His believers, and unbelievers would be shut out. Not knowing what else to do, John fell at the feet of the great angel who had made the announcement. The situation was too tense—what else could he do? Then the angel said...

"Stop...don't worship me; I am just a servant of God like you." John knew that angels were different from humans, but both humans and angels, in their tasks, served God. Angels had also been created by God, just like humans. The great angel said...

"Worship God..."

John continued to precisely write everything that he saw in a book—a book that would give a faithful witness to Jesus Christ, so that all might worship Him.

Then John saw the door to Heaven open. It was the same door that John had seen at the beginning of his vision. When the door opened, John saw a white horse standing there, with Jesus sitting upon it. Because those left on earth might not know Him, the great angel announced the rider of the horse...

"HE IS FAITHFUL AND TRUE...." The eyes of Jesus were bright and scary—they were the eyes of war. They had the intensity of a soldier who takes up his weapon to go into battle. This was not the time for compassion, nor was this the time to show mercy. The writer of Ecclesiastes had said, "There is a time of peace and a time of war, a time to kill and a time to refrain from killing." This was a time of final punishment.

Those on the other side of the battle line had made their choice. Although God loved them, they hated Him in return; and they had made themselves an enemy of God by turning their back on His love. They were more than passive unbelievers; they had clenched their fists to shake them in His face, declaring, "You will not rule my life, You will not have my soul." Those on the other side of the battle line had been hardened in their unbelief. If they could have, they would have done anything to destroy God and His influence in their life. They had rejected His rule over themselves and over the world.

Again, John looked at Jesus prepared for battle, and saw behind Him the armies of Heaven—millions upon millions of soldiers ready for battle, ready to follow Jesus into war. This was a battle they would not lose.

The army waited for the command from their Master. Soon, He would open His mouth, and from it would come the Word of God. All people on earth would be judged by His Word, and they would feel the fierce wrath of Almighty God that had been promised in the Scriptures.

John knew who was riding upon the white horse at the head of the army. It was Jesus, the One who had ridden meekly into Jerusalem on Palm Sunday on a donkey. John knew this was the same Jesus who had come to him on the shore of Lake Galilee, inviting him to "Come, follow Me."

But now, Jesus was called, "KING OF KINGS and LORD OF LORDS." While on earth, Jesus had lived in a nation ruled by a king called Caesar. He had obeyed Caesar's law, stood before Caesar's judgment throne, and was executed by Caesar's soldiers. And as Jesus hung on the cross, it appeared that Caesar was both king and lord. But not on this final day of human history.

Jesus is the King of Caesar…but not just Caesar. Jesus is the King of every king who has ever lived. Jesus is "KING OF KINGS and LORD OF LORDS."

John turned his eyes away; he would not write battle descriptions about the final conflict on earth. He would not list the numbers of those who would die in opposition to Jesus Christ, nor would he describe how they died, nor would he describe the final judgment. He would not describe the blood…gore…squalor…and death. The battle scene would not be written in John's Book of the Revelation. Why glorify war? Why describe corpses and magnify death?

*Why did they not believe…why did they not repent…why did they not accept Jesus Christ?*

As John thought about the millions who would die under God's judgment, he remembered the words he had penned in his Gospel, "For God so loved the world...." All the people in the world were loved by God. God could say that He loved everyone because He allowed His Son to die in the place of all people, even those rebels who would lie dead on the fields of Armageddon. Jesus had died for them, even though they would not believe, nor would they receive salvation. They would waste their lives needlessly because satan would so effectively blind them that they would refused to believe in God and His Son. When they would choose the path of least resistance, they would choose death.

Then John again heard echoes deep within the cave, a sound returning that he had heard a few minutes earlier. The voice came like thunder rumbling down the valley, like a tidal wave rushing from the ocean. He heard the refrains louder than ever before...

"HALLELUJAH!"

## What I Learned From Jesus' Return

I will use the same words to praise God in Heaven that I use on earth.

I will express my worship better with some words, such as the word "HALLELUJAH!"

I know God will reward me when I live for Him and suffer for Him, just as surely as I know God will judge those who disobey and rebel against Him.

I know God will not punish people without first giving them an opportunity to respond.

I can better endure present sufferings when I realize there is a future reward.

## Section Nine

### Scripture: Revelation chapters 19–20

Lord, John heard the roar of a great multitude,
> Shouting, "Hallelujah…victory and glory and power
> To our God."
>> It was all Heaven worshiping You because
>> Christ was getting ready for His return to earth.
> The crowd shouted, "God judges accurately and God punishes fair;
>> He has condemned the religious prostitute
>> Who corrupted mankind with her adultery.
> God has avenged the death of the martyrs
>> That the evil prostitute has killed."

Lord, the crowd sang to You, "Hallelujah…the smoke from
The judgment of the prostitute goes on forever."

> Then the 24 saints before the throne
>> And the four Seraphim around the throne
> Fell on their faces to worship You, the God of judgment,
>> Crying, "AMEN, we agree with Your judgment.
>> AMEN…Your will be done forever."

Lord, a voice echoed out over the multitude,
> "Praise our God, all His servants,
> Great and small who reverence Him."
John heard the immense crowd roar like thunder,
> "Hallelujah…the reign of God over
> The earth is about to begin.
Let us be glad and rejoice because
> The marriage supper of the Lamb is ready;
> Jesus will be united with His Bride, the Church.

The Bride is ready because she is made pure
    By the blood of the Lamb.
She is dressed in fine white linen
    Which is made from the good deeds of the saints."
The angel told John to write, "God has said, 'Blessed are the saints
    Who are invited to the wedding supper of the Lord.'"

Lord, John fell at the feet to worship the angel, but he said,
    "No, don't worship me, I am a servant
    Of God like you; worship God."
The angel explained the purpose of the prophetic words
    He had given John;
    It was to tell all about Jesus.

Lord, John then saw Heaven open, and riding a white horse
    Was Jesus, who is called Faithful and True.
Jesus was ready to make war with all the armies
    Gathered in the valley of Armageddon to oppose
    Him and His plan for the Holy Land.
His eyes as blazing fire saw into the hearts
    And rebellion of all people.
He wore a crown, symbolic of His rulership
    Over all the earth.
He had a name embroidered on His garment
    That no one knew but Him.
The name of Jesus was the Word of God,
    And His garments were covered with the blood
    Of those He had defeated.
An enormous army followed Him;
    They wore white symbolizing their purity,
    And they rode white horses.
Jesus held the sharp sword of justice
    To strike down those who rebelled against Him,
    And He will rule them with an iron grip.

On His robe is written, "King of Kings and Lord of Lords."
      Now He will tread over His enemies
      As grapes are crushed in the wine press.

Lord, John saw an angel standing in the sun,
      Shouting to all the birds of Heaven,
"Come eat the bodies of those
      Who fought against God and His plan."
The dead included all the generals, soldiers,
      Horses, and citizens—great and small.

Lord, John saw the antichrist was taken prisoner
      With the false prophet who had worked miracles,
Deceiving those who were branded with 666,
      And who worshiped the statue of the antichrist.
These two were thrown into the fiery lake
      Burning with brimstone.
All the rest were killed under the judgment of God,
      And the birds had a feast on their flesh.

Lord, next John saw an angel descending from Heaven
      With the key to hell.
He had an enormous chain, and when He
      Overpowered satan, who is also called
      The serpent, the devil, and the dragon,
He chained him and threw him into hell
      To remain there 1,000 years.
Then the angel shut the entrance and sealed it
      To make sure the devil would not
      Deceive people until the 1,000 years were over.
At the end of that time, satan
      Would be released for a short period of time.

Lord, John saw many who had the authority to judge,
      Sitting on judgment thrones.

Then John saw the martyrs resurrected to new life;
    They had been beheaded
    Because of their testimony.
They had not worshiped the beast, or his statue,
    Nor had they been branded in their hearts or forehead
With the brand of the antichrist—666.
    They reigned with Christ 1,000 years.

The unsaved dead were not resurrected yet;
    They were to be judged after the 1,000 years.
The saved are raised in the first resurrection;
    The second death holds no power over them.
They will be priests who worship You for 1,000 years,
    And they will reign with Christ for 1,000 years.
        Amen.

# Section Ten

# SEEING THE FUTURE HEAVEN

## Scripture: Revelation chapters 21–22

John propped his head in his hands, he was weak. The vision of people being cast into hell was distasteful. He didn't want to write about eternal retribution, but he had to write what God commanded. Strength is sapped from people when doing something they don't want to do. John was the apostle of love. He had always appealed to the love of God. But the other side of God was also to be revealed—His holiness and justice. John wrote about hell because he could be trusted to do anything Christ told him to do.

John wrote how millions of unsaved people appeared before God's eternal bar of justice. Then, it was too late to give them a second chance to be saved. Even if God would give them a second chance, they would continue to rebel to the end. The would never repent.

But God never asked, "What sin did you commit?" Their filthiness was no longer the issue. Instead, each, who appeared before God, was asked…

"What have you done with Jesus Christ?"

The books that recorded what each had done on earth were examined. The first book that was opened was called "The Lamb's Book of Life." It contained the names of everyone who had  placed their trust in Jesus Christ for salvation.

During this judgment, when a person appeared before God, a voice rang out…

"Is your name written in the Lamb's Book of Life?"

One after another, they all answered the same, "No!" They could not lie in the presence of God, who is truth. When asked if they believed in Jesus Christ, each answered defiantly…

"NO!"

"Depart from Me," was the only response that God could give. "You never believed in Jesus for salvation." They were then sent to hell, the place prepared for the devil and his angels. The lost didn't plead for a second chance, nor did they weep with remorse. As they had died rejecting eternal life, so they stood defiantly before God continuing their rebellion which had characterized their life. Those who had violently rejected God in life, again violently repudiated God as they stood in judgment. Those who had quietly turned from God in life, again softly turned from God as they stood before the Great White Judgment Throne. Their decision sealed their eternity—they had chosen hell over Heaven.

John's head dropped to the table, his eyelids closed. Although he slept fitfully, dreaming nightmares of the lost, he continued sleeping because he was too weary to fight it off. John had to sleep to regain stamina—he still had another scene to write in his book.

Waking a little while later, John stretched his arms to prepare himself to finish his task. The candle burned low, and he wasn't sure if it was day or night outside his cave. But he would not go to see. He didn't need to know the time of day on Patmos; he was concerned with Heaven. Again, he turned away from the morsel of bread—he would not eat until he finished his book. John looked up to God and asked…

"What happened after the unsaved were judged?"

In answer to his prayer, God gave John a new vision—a vision of Heaven.

John saw the first Heaven and the first earth pass away. All the great building projects were gone…civilizations…libraries…communication marvels…humanitarian efforts—gone.

John wept.

Then John the Seer observed the emergence of a new Heaven, more glorious than the previous. Next he saw a new earth, new in the sense of being transformed and glorified, yet an earth like the former one. This time, however, there was no curse, nor rebellion. The new earth was a city ruled by God. It was prepared for people who would be ruled by God, a place where the renewed beauty of nature was more lovely than the previous earth, for God had transformed the world.

The new heavenly city came down from God—it was a place where God would live with His people. The holy city was the New Jerusalem. John was told the city "was pure like a bride prepared for her husband." Just as the believers were called "the Bride" for Jesus the Bridegroom, so the place they would live was compatible to the purity of the people of God.

John knew that his father and mother were in the new city, for they believed in Jesus. Intuitively, John knew that those of his family and friends who had placed their faith in Jesus would also live there. But thinking of his loved ones also made John remember those who wouldn't be there. John remembered a ruler of the synagogue in Capernaum who had refused to believe Jesus was the Messiah. He wouldn't be in the new city. John remembered some other friends from Jerusalem who also wouldn't be there. In life, they had hardened their hearts to Jesus. Then with hardened faces, they rejected Him in hell, as they had rejected Him on earth.

John wept.

Not only did John cry, but all those in the heavenly city wept when they realized that friends and family were missing. How could they enjoy Heaven with the thought of loved ones not there?

Even in the cave in Patmos, John wept real tears, for the future was as real as the present. But he didn't cry for long, for God came to wipe away tears—all tears. Not just the tears trickling down the deep lines of John's wrinkled face, but God wiped away all tears of all believers in Heaven...for all that caused their sadness.

And with God's eternal handkerchief, He erased from the memories of His people all the thoughts that made them weep. They wouldn't remember their lost friends...that memory was wiped away. They wouldn't remember their sins and failures...those memories were gone. They wouldn't remember sickness...pain...betrayals. Every memory that would destroy their joy and peace was wiped away. All sin was gone, separated from them, as far as the east is from the west. In Heaven there was no sorrow, no sickness, no pain.

## Your Time to Worship

Lord, there were many sins in my life before I was saved, but because You forgave them, I thank You.

Lord, there have been many times I've failed You since I've been saved, but because You put them under the blood of Christ, I praise You.

Lord, there have been many people to whom I haven't witnessed, but because You forgive my lethargy, I magnify You.

Lord, there have been many times I haven't prayed as I should have, but because You wipe away the tears of unfulfilled potential, I worship You.

Lord, there are things I should do today, but still will not have completed at Your return; I continue to pray, "Come quickly."

"Come," the Spirit said to John, "I will show you the center of Heaven and what people will do in Heaven." The Spirit carried John to a high mountain, and from that vantage point, John could see everything in eternity. He was not viewing Heaven with his human eyes, but John saw things through the eyes of the Spirit.

John saw a river, a sparkling clear river flowing through the middle of Heaven. Every city in the ancient world had been built on a river or well; without water, there would have been no life. Likewise, Heaven would have all the water its inhabitants needed, but they wouldn't need to drink water to live. They had already drank from the water offered to the woman at the well by Jesus. "Whoever drinks of the water that I shall give him will never thirst. But the water that I shall give him will become in him a fountain of water springing up into everlasting life" (John 4:14).

Then the Spirit told John, "The people of Heaven don't need to drink to live, but many in Heaven will drink for enjoyment and refreshment."

John looked up the river to see its source and noticed that it was coming from the throne of God and the Lamb. The water came from God Himself. As the river flowed through Heaven, John observed trees growing near the bank on both sides of the river, just as trees on earth had grown near water so their roots could drink. These trees looked similar to the trees of earth, but their fruit was different. The Spirit explained to John that the trees had 12 different kinds of fruit on each tree, and they produced a crop of ripe fruit for each month, not like earthly trees that had produced a crop only once a year. The inhabitants of Heaven would never be hungry, neither would they become bored eating the same kind of food all the time. Abundant fruit continually!

"Will there be enough fruit?" John asked.

"You do not have to eat in Heaven," the Spirit explained. "Because all believers have eternal bodies, food is not required. But if you choose to eat for enjoyment, there will be enough for all."

"Will we sleep in Heaven?" John asked.

"There is no night in Heaven," the Spirit answered. "You won't need a candle, because the Lord will be your light. Sleep is not required because no one will get tired, nor will they get sick. The night was made for sleeping on earth, but people in Heaven will sleep only if they choose."

"Will we know everyone in Heaven?" John asked.

The Spirit smiled because John in his old age was having trouble remembering some of his friends. John had even forgotten what he wrote in his letter about Heaven, "We shall know as we are known." Then the Spirit explained, "You will recognize people as you remembered them. Those you knew on earth, you will know in Heaven. You will not know everyone. Only God knows all things." The Spirit explained to John that he would know all the people in Heaven he needed to know.

"Will I learn things in Heaven and will I grow wiser?" John asked the Spirit.

"Yes..." the Spirit explained the leaves of the trees were for the growth of believers. "You will continually grow in knowledge as you grew on the earth, but you won't learn everything there is to know. Only God knows all things. You will continue to learn things throughout eternity and still never learn everything there is to know."

"Will I work in Heaven?" The ever-curious John continued asking questions of the Spirit.

"Yes..." the Spirit again answered. "All God's servants will minister to Him in worship." The Spirit explained that just as people were created to glorify and worship God on earth, so their task in Heaven would be to give glory and worship to God.

John remembered there was no sin in Heaven and no one would have a sin nature. No one would hate work in Heaven as people hated working here on earth. Those Christians who didn't want to worship God on earth, or didn't do it very often, will all worship God passionately in Heaven. There would be no temptation to by-pass worship. God's people would instinctively return to worship God again...and again...and again. The Spirit explained...

"You will work, you will desire to work, you will grow in maturity from your work, and you will never reach a plateau where you'll stop growing in character and grace. In Heaven, you will continually grow to be like Jesus."

John viewed Heaven from the top of a high mountain, watching people go about their duties. He saw where people lived—the mansions promised by Jesus, and he saw them fellowshipping together. Heaven was a desirable place. Then he commented...

"Life in Heaven is not unlike life on earth."

The Spirit agreed with John's observation, then added, "Why would God create life in the garden of Eden, then change His plans to give a completely different kind of life in Heaven?" The angel noted that God is the same...angels are the same...people are the same; so why then should life be different in Heaven?

John agreed with the Spirit, but he didn't like waiting for this beautiful place. He prayed, "Lord, come now to end Roman persecution of the Church." He wanted Heaven now. God answered...

"Jesus will come soon, but no one knows the hour that He will come...not the angels...not the elders...not the Seraphim." The Lord explained that Jesus would come when people least expected Him...like a thief in the night.

"What will happen to followers who are suffering at the hand of Rome?" John couldn't forget he was in prison at Patmos. He couldn't forget that his brothers—the other apostles—had been violently killed. "Why can't You come now?"

The Spirit explained that the Great Commission still required them to preach the Gospel to the ends of the earth...they hadn't done that yet. The Spirit explained that as a great harvest of evangelism continued, "The devil will continue to persecute the Church, and those addicted to filthiness will continue to be filthy." The Spirit directed His attention to the Church, "Let the believers who live holy lives, continue to be holy."

Jesus was listening to the conversation between John and the Spirit, because Jesus knows everything, and He whispered in John's ear, "Behold, I come quickly, bringing a reward for every believer according to their faithfulness."

John returned to his crude table to write the things he saw in Heaven. He wrote furiously...as fervently as a man past 90 could write, and littered the floor of the cave with pages of the book. Soon John would finish and gather the pages in order. In his heart, he knew his book would not be destroyed by his Roman guards, nor would it be lost at sea by those who might escape to deliver it to the world.

Because the Lord Jesus Christ had commanded him to write...because the Holy Spirit had inspired its inscription...because the Father had revealed its content to him, John knew his book called The Revelation would be first delivered to the prisoners waiting at the mouth of the cave, then to encourage the Church in persecution all over the Roman Empire, and finally to the future believers who needed to know about the coming events and about Heaven itself.

John looked at the white cloth covering the morsel of bread. "Should I eat now?" John wondered if he were finished writing the book. He would not feed his body until he fed the world with the bread of God.

"The Spirit and the Bride invite all to come to God."

Hearing the invitation, John slipped from the table to the floor. He bowed in humility before God, not to worship this time, but to intercede for lost people to come to God. As he prayed, John heard...

"Let all who hear the Word of God come..."

John continued interceding when he again heard the invitation...

"Let him who is thirsty come to drink of the water of God."

When the Lord stopped speaking to John, the ancient apostle arose from prayer, his knees throbbing. Again John sat at his table. Then the Lord gave John further instructions to write in his book...

"If any one hears the prophecies of this book and adds to them, I will give him more punishment than is written in this book."

John wrote the sentence just as the Lord dictated it. Then God spoke again...

"If anyone takes away any words from this book, I will take away his part out of the Book of Life."

John knew he was coming to the end of the book. He bowed his head at the table to ask, "Is there anything else?" Jesus, who came to John in the cave when he began the book, returned. Jesus understood the heart's passion of John and spoke His final words to him...

"Surely, I come quickly."

John wrote the last words of Jesus, then added his own prayer, "Even so, come, Lord Jesus."

Now, John had come to the end, and added the benediction, "The grace of our Lord Jesus Christ be with you all. Amen."

John finished writing and squeezed the last drop of ink from his quill. He gathered the pages, placing them in order. Uncovering the morsel of bread, John lifted his eyes to Heaven, gave thanks, and ate.

## What I Learned About Heaven

I will go to live with God in Heaven if I have believed in Christ as my personal Savior.

I should attempt to win as many to salvation as possible, because there will be no second chances after death or the return of Christ.

I will weep in Heaven for my friends who are lost, but God will wipe away all tears and make me forget.

I will live a life in Heaven that is not much different from life on earth.

I will learn, grow, and develop in Heaven.

## Section Ten

## Chapters 21–22

Lord, You showed the new Heaven and the new Earth
> To John because the first Heaven and earth
Were burnt up in the fervent heat.
> The new earth didn't have any seas.
John saw the holy city—the new Jerusalem
> Coming down from Your presence in Heaven,
> As beautiful as a bride at a wedding.
Then John heard a loud voice announcing,
> "God is now making His home among people.
He will live among them,
> And they will be His people.
He will wipe away every tear from their eyes.
> There will be no more death, sickness, or pain;
> All sorrows of the past are gone."

Lord, You who sits on the throne announced,
> "I am making everything new!"
Then You told John, "Write this down,
> For this is the way it will happen."
Just as Christ on the cross said of sin, "It is finished,"
> So You will say of life on this earth,
> "It is finished."

Then Jesus said, "I am the Alpha and Omega,
> I am the beginning of all things, and
> I am the purpose of all things.
I will give water from the well of eternal life
> To anyone who thirsts for Me.
> This is My gift to those who are victorious.

They will be Your children, O Father in Heaven,
    And You will be their God;
But You reserve the lake of fire for
    Unbelievers, cowards, those speaking
    Obscenities, murderers, sex offenders,
Idolaters, and all liars—
    That will be their second death."

Lord, one of the seven angels with bowls of judgment
    Said to John, "Come, I will show you the Bride,
    The wife of the Lamb."
Then John was carried away in a prophetic vision
    To a high mountain where he saw the new Jerusalem,
    The holy city coming down from God.
It was filled with the Shekinah glory of God,
    And it sparkled like a dish of precious jewels,
    And it was crystal clear.
The walls were very high and very wide,
    And there were 12 gates, guarded by 12 angels.
The names of the 12 tribes of Israel
    Were written on the 12 gates.
There were three gates on each side—
    North, South, East, and West.
The walls were built on 12 foundation stones,
    And the names were written on them
    Of the 12 apostles who had followed Jesus.
The angel held in his hand a golden
    Rod to measure the city and walls.
He measured 1500 miles from side to side
    And from top to bottom.
The city was foursquare, as long
    As it is wide, and it is high.
Next he measured the thickness of the walls;
    They were 216 feet across,

According to his measurement.
The city was constructed of transparent gold;
One could see through it like glass.
The walls were like jasper;
The 12 foundations were garnished with jewels.
The first foundation was like jasper,
The second foundation was like sapphire,
The third foundation was like chalcedony,
The fourth foundation was like emerald,.
The fifth foundation was like sardonyx,
The sixth foundation was like sardius,
The seventh foundation was like chrysolite,
The eighth foundation was like beryl,
The ninth foundation was like topaz,
The tenth foundation was like chrysoprase,
The eleventh foundation was like jacinth,
The twelfth foundation was like amethyst,

The 12 gates glistened like a pearl,
And the streets were paved with pure gold,
As clear as transparent glass.

There was no temple in the city, because people
Worshiped You and the Lamb everywhere.
The city did not need sun or moon for light,
Because it was continually lit by
Your Shekinah glory and the Lamb.
The people who are saved will walk in the light,
And everyone—including all kings—will glorify You.
The gates will never be shut; they remain open
For there is no night there.
Nothing sinful will enter the city; no one
Who is filthy or lies
Will be allowed in the city.

The only ones there will be true believers
>> Whose names are written in the Lamb's Book of Life.

Lord, the angel showed John a sparkling clean river,
>> Flowing from Your throne and the Lamb.
> It flowed down the middle of the central street of Heaven.
>> Trees of Life grew on each side of the river,
> And a new crop of fruit grew each month
>> That could be harvested each month.
> The leaves provided growth for all people
>> Who will eat from the Trees of Life.

Lord, there is nothing evil in the city,
>> Because Your throne and the Lamb are there.
>> All Your servants will worship You continually.
> Your servants will see the face of the Lamb,
>> And His name will be on their forehead.
> There will be no night—no need for lights—for You
> Will give light to the city.
>> And You will rule Your people forever.

Lord, the angel told John, "God's people can trust
>> These words and descriptions of Heaven.
>> Be prepared, He is coming soon."
> You who tell the future to Your prophets
>> Sent your angel to tell John these things that will soon occur.
> They are blessed who read this book
>> And believe what it says.

Lord, when John saw and heard all these things that
>> Were about to happen, he lay prostrate
>> To worship the angel who showed him these things.
> The angel said, "No! I am a servant of Jesus
>> Like you are. Obey what prophets say,
>> 'Worship God!'"

The angel instructed John not to close
  The book he was writing,
    But tell everyone its message
Because the evil person will continue to do evil
    And the filthy will continue to do filthy things.
Also good people will continue to do good,
    And holy people will continue being holy.

Lord, Jesus said, "I am coming soon, and I'll
    Have a reward for everyone,
      According to the deeds they have done."
"I am Alpha and Omega, the Beginning and the End,
    The First and Last of everything.
Those who live by My Word
    Can enter the gates into the city,
      And eat the fruit of the Tree of Life."
Outside the city there will be rebels, and sorcerers,
    And the sexually impure, murderers,
      Idolaters, and those who love to lie.
Jesus sent an angel to tell John
    These messages for the churches.
Jesus was born in the family line of David.
    He is the bright Star of the morning.

Lord, the Holy Spirit and all believers
  Tell the unsaved, "Come!"
    Let all those who are thirsty, "Come!"
  All who want the water of eternal life
    May have it free.

Lord, John warned everyone who read this book,
      Don't add anything to this book, or God
      Will add to their punishment.
  And if any take away from the things in this book,
      God will take away their part in the Book of Life

And in the holy city.
Jesus who repeated the warnings said,
    "Surely I come quickly!"
John agreed with Jesus and said, "Amen!
    Even so, come, Lord Jesus."
Then John gave the benediction, "The grace
    Of our Lord Jesus Christ be with you."
            Amen.

# EPILOGUE

John did not die on Patmos, nor was his manuscript lost. In the affairs of man, Domitian died (A.D. 96 ), and persecution against the Church subsided. In the sovereignty of God, the aged apostle was released from Patmos. John sailed from the island with only the clothes on his back and a large sack containing his handwritten manuscript that he carefully protected from the salt air of the Aegean Sea. He returned to his beloved church in Ephesus, where he sat at a large table at the front of the crowded room to read *The Revelation* to those who had been persecuted for their faith. The book was addressed to seven churches, Ephesus being named first. Young scribes in the Ephesian church made copies for the other churches, then delivered them to their destination. News spread rapidly throughout the other churches of Asia Minor (today's Turkey) about John's book that told about the future. Other churches sent scribes—usually young men preparing for the ministry—to Ephesus where they carefully copied every word. Returning home, the book was read to the church. *The Revelation* was again copied by other young scribes to be carried to an ever-widening circle of influence.

The readers of the early Church struggled to understand the obscure reference to seals...wrath...antichrist...and the interpretation of a hundred other symbols that were coming in the future. But by faith they believed the future would happen just the way John described it; and as the future judgment got closer, the message of the Book would be clear to those for whom it was written. But one thing was immediately clear to the early Church—and today's Church—Jesus will be with us in persecution...Jesus will come for us...Jesus will reward us in the future, and there is a wonderful place called Heaven where we all will live eternally. The early

Church read about the coming Heaven, and rejoiced in its surety. As they read, they prayed the same as John,

*"Even so, come, Lord Jesus."*

The End—which is, The Beginning.

# Appendix A

# THE BOOK OF REVELATION

## KING JAMES VERSION OF THE BIBLE

### Chapter 1

[1] The Revelation of Jesus Christ, which God gave unto him, to shew unto his servants things which must shortly come to pass; and he sent and signified it by his angel unto his servant John:

[2] Who bare record of the word of God, and of the testimony of Jesus Christ, and of all things that he saw.

[3] Blessed is he that readeth, and they that hear the words of this prophecy, and keep those things which are written therein: for the time is at hand.

[4] John to the seven churches which are in Asia: Grace be unto you, and peace, from him which is, and which was, and which is to come; and from the seven Spirits which are before his throne;

[5] And from Jesus Christ, who is the faithful witness, and the first begotten of the dead, and the prince of the kings of the earth. Unto him that loved us, and washed us from our sins in his own blood,

[6] And hath made us kings and priests unto God and his Father; to him be glory and dominion for ever and ever. Amen.

[7] Behold, he cometh with clouds; and every eye shall see him, and they also which pierced him: and all kindreds of the earth shall wail because of him. Even so, Amen.

[8] I am Alpha and Omega, the beginning and the ending, saith the Lord, which is, and which was, and which is to come, the Almighty.

[9] I John, who also am your brother, and companion in tribulation, and in the kingdom and patience of Jesus Christ, was in the isle that is called Patmos, for the word of God, and for the testimony of Jesus Christ.

[10] I was in the Spirit on the Lord's day, and heard behind me a great voice, as of a trumpet,

[11] Saying, I am Alpha and Omega, the first and the last: and, What thou seest, write in a book, and send it unto the seven churches which are in Asia; unto Ephesus, and unto Smyrna, and unto Pergamos, and unto Thyatira, and unto Sardis, and unto Philadelphia, and unto Laodicea.

[12] And I turned to see the voice that spake with me. And being turned, I saw seven golden candlesticks;

[13] And in the midst of the seven candlesticks one like unto the Son of man, clothed with a garment down to the foot, and girt about the paps with a golden girdle.

[14] His head and his hairs were white like wool, as white as snow; and his eyes were as a flame of fire;

[15] And his feet like unto fine brass, as if they burned in a furnace; and his voice as the sound of many waters.

[16] And he had in his right hand seven stars: and out of his mouth went a sharp twoedged sword: and his countenance was as the sun shineth in his strength.

[17] And when I saw him, I fell at his feet as dead. And he laid his right hand upon me, saying unto me, Fear not; I am the first and the last:

[18] I am he that liveth, and was dead; and, behold, I am alive for evermore, Amen; and have the keys of hell and of death.

[19] Write the things which thou hast seen, and the things which are, and the things which shall be hereafter;

[20] The mystery of the seven stars which thou sawest in my right hand, and the seven golden candlesticks. The seven stars are the angels of the seven churches: and the seven candlesticks which thou sawest are the seven churches.

## Chapter 2

[1] Unto the angel of the church of Ephesus write; These things saith he that holdeth the seven stars in his right hand, who walketh in the midst of the seven golden candlesticks;

[2] I know thy works, and thy labour, and thy patience, and how thou canst not bear them which are evil: and thou hast tried them which say they are apostles, and are not, and hast found them liars:

[3] And hast borne, and hast patience, and for my name's sake hast laboured, and hast not fainted.

[4] Nevertheless I have somewhat against thee, because thou hast left thy first love.

[5] Remember therefore from whence thou art fallen, and repent, and do the first works; or else I will come unto thee quickly, and will remove thy candlestick out of his place, except thou repent.

[6] But this thou hast, that thou hatest the deeds of the Nicolaitans, which I also hate.

[7] He that hath an ear, let him hear what the Spirit saith unto the churches; To him that overcometh will I give to eat of the tree of life, which is in the midst of the paradise of God.

[8] And unto the angel of the church in Smyrna write; These things saith the first and the last, which was dead, and is alive;

[9] I know thy works, and tribulation, and poverty, (but thou art rich) and I know the blasphemy of them which say they are Jews, and are not, but are the synagogue of Satan.

[10] Fear none of those things which thou shalt suffer: behold, the devil shall cast some of you into prison, that ye may be tried; and ye shall

have tribulation ten days: be thou faithful unto death, and I will give thee a crown of life.

[11] He that hath an ear, let him hear what the Spirit saith unto the churches; He that overcometh shall not be hurt of the second death.

[12] And to the angel of the church in Pergamos write; These things saith he which hath the sharp sword with two edges;

[13] I know thy works, and where thou dwellest, even where Satan's seat is: and thou holdest fast my name, and hast not denied my faith, even in those days wherein Antipas was my faithful martyr, who was slain among you, where Satan dwelleth.

[14] But I have a few things against thee, because thou hast there them that hold the doctrine of Balaam, who taught Balac to cast a stumblingblock before the children of Israel, to eat things sacrificed unto idols, and to commit fornication.

[15] So hast thou also them that hold the doctrine of the Nicolaitans, which thing I hate.

[16] Repent; or else I will come unto thee quickly, and will fight against them with the sword of my mouth.

[17] He that hath an ear, let him hear what the Spirit saith unto the churches; To him that overcometh will I give to eat of the hidden manna, and will give him a white stone, and in the stone a new name written, which no man knoweth saving he that receiveth it.

[18] And unto the angel of the church in Thyatira write; These things saith the Son of God, who hath his eyes like unto a flame of fire, and his feet are like fine brass;

[19] I know thy works, and charity, and service, and faith, and thy patience, and thy works; and the last to be more than the first.

[20] Notwithstanding I have a few things against thee, because thou sufferest that woman Jezebel, which calleth herself a prophetess, to teach and to seduce my servants to commit fornication, and to eat things sacrificed unto idols.

[21] And I gave her space to repent of her fornication; and she repented not.

[22] Behold, I will cast her into a bed, and them that commit adultery with her into great tribulation, except they repent of their deeds.

[23] And I will kill her children with death; and all the churches shall know that I am he which searcheth the reins and hearts: and I will give unto every one of you according to your works.

[24] But unto you I say, and unto the rest in Thyatira, as many as have not this doctrine, and which have not known the depths of Satan, as they speak; I will put upon you none other burden.

[25] But that which ye have already hold fast till I come.

[26] And he that overcometh, and keepeth my works unto the end, to him will I give power over the nations:

[27] And he shall rule them with a rod of iron; as the vessels of a potter shall they be broken to shivers: even as I received of my Father.

[28] And I will give him the morning star.

[29] He that hath an ear, let him hear what the Spirit saith unto the churches.

## Chapter 3

[1] And unto the angel of the church in Sardis write; These things saith he that hath the seven Spirits of God, and the seven stars; I know thy works, that thou hast a name that thou livest, and art dead.

[2] Be watchful, and strengthen the things which remain, that are ready to die: for I have not found thy works perfect before God.

[3] Remember therefore how thou hast received and heard, and hold fast, and repent. If therefore thou shalt not watch, I will come on thee as a thief, and thou shalt not know what hour I will come upon thee.

[4] Thou hast a few names even in Sardis which have not defiled their garments; and they shall walk with me in white: for they are worthy.

[5] He that overcometh, the same shall be clothed in white raiment; and I will not blot out his name out of the book of life, but I will confess his name before my Father, and before his angels.

[6] He that hath an ear, let him hear what the Spirit saith unto the churches.

[7] And to the angel of the church in Philadelphia write; These things saith he that is holy, he that is true, he that hath the key of David, he that

openeth, and no man shutteth; and shutteth, and no man openeth;

[8] I know thy works: behold, I have set before thee an open door, and no man can shut it: for thou hast a little strength, and hast kept my word, and hast not denied my name.

[9] Behold, I will make them of the synagogue of Satan, which say they are Jews, and are not, but do lie; behold, I will make them to come and worship before thy feet, and to know that I have loved thee.

[10] Because thou hast kept the word of my patience, I also will keep thee from the hour of temptation, which shall come upon all the world, to try them that dwell upon the earth.

[11] Behold, I come quickly: hold that fast which thou hast, that no man take thy crown.

[12] Him that overcometh will I make a pillar in the temple of my God, and he shall go no more out: and I will write upon him the name of my God, and the name of the city of my God, which is new Jerusalem, which cometh down out of heaven from my God: and I will write upon him my new name.

[13] He that hath an ear, let him hear what the Spirit saith unto the churches.

[14] And unto the angel of the church of the Laodiceans write; These things saith the Amen, the faithful and true witness, the beginning of the creation of God;

[15] I know thy works, that thou art neither cold nor hot: I would thou wert cold or hot.

[16] So then because thou art luke-warm, and neither cold nor hot, I will spue thee out of my mouth.

[17] Because thou sayest, I am rich, and increased with goods, and have need of nothing; and knowest not that thou art wretched, and miserable, and poor, and blind, and naked:

[18] I counsel thee to buy of me gold tried in the fire, that thou mayest be rich; and white raiment, that thou mayest be clothed, and that the shame of thy nakedness do not appear; and anoint thine eyes with eyesalve, that thou mayest see.

[19] As many as I love, I rebuke and chasten: be zealous therefore, and repent.

[20] Behold, I stand at the door, and knock: if any man hear my voice, and open the door, I will come in to him, and will sup with him, and he with me.

[21] To him that overcometh will I grant to sit with me in my throne, even as I also overcame, and am set down with my Father in his throne.

[22] He that hath an ear, let him hear what the Spirit saith unto the churches.

## Chapter 4

[1] After this I looked, and, behold, a door was opened in heaven: and the first voice which I heard was as it were of a trumpet talking with me; which said, Come up hither, and I will shew thee things which must be hereafter.

[2] And immediately I was in the spirit: and, behold, a throne was set in heaven, and one sat on the throne.

[3] And he that sat was to look upon like a jasper and a sardine stone: and there was a rainbow round about the throne, in sight like unto an emerald.

[4] And round about the throne were four and twenty seats: and upon the seats I saw four and twenty elders sitting, clothed in white raiment; and they had on their heads crowns of gold.

[5] And out of the throne proceeded lightnings and thunderings and voices: and there were seven lamps of fire burning before the throne, which are the seven Spirits of God.

[6] And before the throne there was a sea of glass like unto crystal: and in the midst of the throne, and round about the throne, were four beasts full of eyes before and behind.

[7] And the first beast was like a lion, and the second beast like a calf, and the third beast had a face as a man, and the fourth beast was like a flying eagle.

[8] And the four beasts had each of them six wings about him; and they were full of eyes within: and they rest not day and night, saying, Holy, holy, holy, Lord God Almighty, which was, and is, and is to come.

[9] And when those beasts give glory and honour and thanks to him that sat on the throne, who liveth for ever and ever,

[10] The four and twenty elders fall down before him that sat on the throne, and worship him that liveth

THE BOOK OF REVELATION—KJV

for ever and ever, and cast their crowns before the throne, saying,

[11] Thou art worthy, O Lord, to receive glory and honour and power: for thou hast created all things, and for thy pleasure they are and were created.

## Chapter 5

[1] And I saw in the right hand of him that sat on the throne a book written within and on the backside, sealed with seven seals.

[2] And I saw a strong angel proclaiming with a loud voice, Who is worthy to open the book, and to loose the seals thereof?

[3] And no man in heaven, nor in earth, neither under the earth, was able to open the book, neither to look thereon.

[4] And I wept much, because no man was found worthy to open and to read the book, neither to look thereon.

[5] And one of the elders saith unto me, Weep not: behold, the Lion of the tribe of Juda, the Root of David, hath prevailed to open the book, and to loose the seven seals thereof.

[6] And I beheld, and, lo, in the midst of the throne and of the four beasts, and in the midst of the elders, stood a Lamb as it had been slain, having seven horns and seven eyes, which are the seven Spirits of God sent forth into all the earth.

[7] And he came and took the book out of the right hand of him that sat upon the throne.

[8] And when he had taken the book, the four beasts and four and twenty elders fell down before the Lamb, having every one of them harps, and golden vials full of odours, which are the prayers of saints.

[9] And they sung a new song, saying, Thou art worthy to take the book, and to open the seals thereof: for thou wast slain, and hast redeemed us to God by thy blood out of every kindred, and tongue, and people, and nation;

[10] And hast made us unto our God kings and priests: and we shall reign on the earth.

[11] And I beheld, and I heard the voice of many angels round about the throne and the beasts and the elders: and the number of them was ten thousand times ten thousand, and thousands of thousands;

[12] Saying with a loud voice, Worthy is the Lamb that was slain to receive power, and riches, and wisdom, and strength, and honour, and glory, and blessing.

[13] And every creature which is in heaven, and on the earth, and under the earth, and such as are in the sea, and all that are in them, heard I saying, Blessing, and honour, and glory, and power, be unto him that sitteth upon the throne, and unto the Lamb for ever and ever.

[14] And the four beasts said, Amen. And the four and twenty elders fell down and worshipped him that liveth for ever and ever.

## Chapter 6

[1] And I saw when the Lamb opened one of the seals, and I heard, as it were the noise of thunder, one of the four beasts saying, Come and see.

[2] And I saw, and behold a white horse: and he that sat on him had a bow; and a crown was given unto him: and he went forth conquering, and to conquer.

[3] And when he had opened the second seal, I heard the second beast say, Come and see.

[4] And there went out another horse that was red: and power was given to him that sat thereon to take peace from the earth, and that they should kill one another: and there was given unto him a great sword.

[5] And when he had opened the third seal, I heard the third beast say, Come and see. And I beheld, and lo a black horse; and he that sat on him had a pair of balances in his hand.

[6] And I heard a voice in the midst of the four beasts say, A measure of wheat for a penny, and three measures of barley for a penny; and see thou hurt not the oil and the wine.

[7] And when he had opened the fourth seal, I heard the voice of the fourth beast say, Come and see.

[8] And I looked, and behold a pale horse: and his name that sat on him was Death, and Hell followed with him. And power was given unto them over the fourth part of the earth, to kill with sword, and with hunger, and with death, and with the beasts of the earth.

[9] And when he had opened the fifth seal, I saw under the altar the souls of them that were slain for the word of God, and for the testimony which they held:

[10] And they cried with a loud voice, saying, How long, O Lord, holy and true, dost thou not judge and avenge our blood on them that dwell on the earth?

[11] And white robes were given unto every one of them; and it was said unto them, that they should rest yet for a little season, until their fellowservants also and their brethren, that should be killed as they were, should be fulfilled.

[12] And I beheld when he had opened the sixth seal, and, lo, there was a great earthquake; and the sun became black as sackcloth of hair, and the moon became as blood;

[13] And the stars of heaven fell unto the earth, even as a fig tree casteth her untimely figs, when she is shaken of a mighty wind.

[14] And the heaven departed as a scroll when it is rolled together; and every mountain and island were moved out of their places.

[15] And the kings of the earth, and the great men, and the rich men, and the chief captains, and the mighty men, and every bondman, and every free man, hid themselves in the dens and in the rocks of the mountains;

[16] And said to the mountains and rocks, Fall on us, and hide us from the face of him that sitteth on the throne, and from the wrath of the Lamb:

[17] For the great day of his wrath is come; and who shall be able to stand?

## Chapter 7

[1] And after these things I saw four angels standing on the four corners of the earth, holding the four winds of the earth, that the wind should not blow on the earth, nor on the sea, nor on any tree.

[2] And I saw another angel ascending from the east, having the seal of the living God: and he cried with a loud voice to the four angels, to whom it was given to hurt the earth and the sea,

[3] Saying, Hurt not the earth, neither the sea, nor the trees, till we have sealed the servants of our God in their foreheads.

[4] And I heard the number of them which were sealed: and there were sealed an hundred and forty and four thousand of all the tribes of the children of Israel.

[5] Of the tribe of Juda were sealed twelve thousand. Of the tribe of Reuben were sealed twelve thousand. Of the tribe of Gad were sealed twelve thousand.

[6] Of the tribe of Aser were sealed twelve thousand. Of the tribe of Nepthalim were sealed twelve thousand. Of the tribe of Manasses were sealed twelve thousand.

[7] Of the tribe of Simeon were sealed twelve thousand. Of the tribe of Levi were sealed twelve thousand. Of the

tribe of Issachar were sealed twelve thousand.

[8] Of the tribe of Zabulon were sealed twelve thousand. Of the tribe of Joseph were sealed twelve thousand. Of the tribe of Benjamin were sealed twelve thousand.

[9] After this I beheld, and, lo, a great multitude, which no man could number, of all nations, and kindreds, and people, and tongues, stood before the throne, and before the Lamb, clothed with white robes, and palms in their hands;

[10] And cried with a loud voice, saying, Salvation to our God which sitteth upon the throne, and unto the Lamb.

[11] And all the angels stood round about the throne, and about the elders and the four beasts, and fell before the throne on their faces, and worshipped God,

[12] Saying, Amen: Blessing, and glory, and wisdom, and thanksgiving, and honour, and power, and might, be unto our God for ever and ever. Amen.

[13] And one of the elders answered, saying unto me, What are these which are arrayed in white robes? and whence came they?

[14] And I said unto him, Sir, thou knowest. And he said to me, These are they which came out of great tribulation, and have washed their robes, and made them white in the blood of the Lamb.

[15] Therefore are they before the throne of God, and serve him day and night in his temple: and he that

sitteth on the throne shall dwell among them.

[16] They shall hunger no more, neither thirst any more; neither shall the sun light on them, nor any heat.

[17] For the Lamb which is in the midst of the throne shall feed them, and shall lead them unto living fountains of waters: and God shall wipe away all tears from their eyes.

## Chapter 8

[1] And when he had opened the seventh seal, there was silence in heaven about the space of half an hour.

[2] And I saw the seven angels which stood before God; and to them were given seven trumpets.

[3] And another angel came and stood at the altar, having a golden censer; and there was given unto him much incense, that he should offer it with the prayers of all saints upon the golden altar which was before the throne.

[4] And the smoke of the incense, which came with the prayers of the saints, ascended up before God out of the angel's hand.

[5] And the angel took the censer, and filled it with fire of the altar, and cast it into the earth: and there were voices, and thunderings, and lightnings, and an earthquake.

[6] And the seven angels which had the seven trumpets prepared themselves to sound.

[7] The first angel sounded, and there followed hail and fire mingled with blood, and they were cast upon the earth: and the third part of trees was burnt up, and all green grass was burnt up.

[8] And the second angel sounded, and as it were a great mountain burning with fire was cast into the sea: and the third part of the sea became blood;

[9] And the third part of the creatures which were in the sea, and had life, died; and the third part of the ships were destroyed.

[10] And the third angel sounded, and there fell a great star from heaven, burning as it were a lamp, and it fell upon the third part of the rivers, and upon the fountains of waters;

[11] And the name of the star is called Wormwood: and the third part of the waters became wormwood; and many men died of the waters, because they were made bitter.

[12] And the fourth angel sounded, and the third part of the sun was smitten, and the third part of the moon, and the third part of the stars; so as the third part of them was darkened, and the day shone not for a third part of it, and the night likewise.

[13] And I beheld, and heard an angel flying through the midst of heaven, saying with a loud voice, Woe, woe, woe, to the inhabiters of the earth by reason of the other voices of the trumpet of the three angels, which are yet to sound!

## Chapter 9

[1] And the fifth angel sounded, and I saw a star fall from heaven unto the earth: and to him was given the key of the bottomless pit.

[2] And he opened the bottomless pit; and there arose a smoke out of the pit, as the smoke of a great furnace; and the sun and the air were darkened by reason of the smoke of the pit.

[3] And there came out of the smoke locusts upon the earth: and unto them was given power, as the scorpions of the earth have power.

[4] And it was commanded them that they should not hurt the grass of the earth, neither any green thing, neither any tree; but only those men which have not the seal of God in their foreheads.

[5] And to them it was given that they should not kill them, but that they should be tormented five months: and their torment was as the torment of a scorpion, when he striketh a man.

[6] And in those days shall men seek death, and shall not find it; and shall desire to die, and death shall flee from them.

[7] And the shapes of the locusts were like unto horses prepared unto battle; and on their heads were as it were crowns like gold, and their faces were as the faces of men.

[8] And they had hair as the hair of women, and their teeth were as the teeth of lions.

[9] And they had breastplates, as it were breastplates of iron; and the sound of their wings was as the sound of chariots of many horses running to battle.

[10] And they had tails like unto scorpions, and there were stings in their tails: and their power was to hurt men five months.

[11] And they had a king over them, which is the angel of the bottomless pit, whose name in the Hebrew tongue is Abaddon, but in the Greek tongue hath his name Apollyon.

[12] One woe is past; and, behold, there come two woes more hereafter.

[13] And the sixth angel sounded, and I heard a voice from the four horns of the golden altar which is before God,

[14] Saying to the sixth angel which had the trumpet, Loose the four angels which are bound in the great river Euphrates.

[15] And the four angels were loosed, which were prepared for an hour, and a day, and a month, and a year, for to slay the third part of men.

[16] And the number of the army of the horsemen were two hundred thousand thousand: and I heard the number of them.

[17] And thus I saw the horses in the vision, and them that sat on them, having breastplates of fire, and of jacinth, and brimstone: and the heads of the horses were as the heads of lions; and out of their mouths issued fire and smoke and brimstone.

[18] By these three was the third part of men killed, by the fire, and by the

smoke, and by the brimstone, which issued out of their mouths.

[19] For their power is in their mouth, and in their tails: for their tails were like unto serpents, and had heads, and with them they do hurt.

[20] And the rest of the men which were not killed by these plagues yet repented not of the works of their hands, that they should not worship devils, and idols of gold, and silver, and brass, and stone, and of wood: which neither can see, nor hear, nor walk:

[21] Neither repented they of their murders, nor of their sorceries, nor of their fornication, nor of their thefts.

## Chapter 10

[1] And I saw another mighty angel come down from heaven, clothed with a cloud: and a rainbow was upon his head, and his face was as it were the sun, and his feet as pillars of fire:

[2] And he had in his hand a little book open: and he set his right foot upon the sea, and his left foot on the earth,

[3] And cried with a loud voice, as when a lion roareth: and when he had cried, seven thunders uttered their voices.

[4] And when the seven thunders had uttered their voices, I was about to write: and I heard a voice from heaven saying unto me, Seal up those things which the seven thunders uttered, and write them not.

[5] And the angel which I saw stand upon the sea and upon the earth lifted up his hand to heaven,

[6] And sware by him that liveth for ever and ever, who created heaven, and the things that therein are, and the earth, and the things that therein are, and the sea, and the things which are therein, that there should be time no longer:

[7] But in the days of the voice of the seventh angel, when he shall begin to sound, the mystery of God should be finished, as he hath declared to his servants the prophets.

[8] And the voice which I heard from heaven spake unto me again, and said, Go and take the little book which is open in the hand of the angel which standeth upon the sea and upon the earth.

[9] And I went unto the angel, and said unto him, Give me the little book. And he said unto me, Take it, and eat it up; and it shall make thy belly bitter, but it shall be in thy mouth sweet as honey.

[10] And I took the little book out of the angel's hand, and ate it up; and it was in my mouth sweet as honey: and as soon as I had eaten it, my belly was bitter.

[11] And he said unto me, Thou must prophesy again before many peoples, and nations, and tongues, and kings.

## Chapter 11

[1] And there was given me a reed like unto a rod: and the angel stood, saying, Rise, and measure the temple of

God, and the altar, and them that worship therein.

[2] But the court which is without the temple leave out, and measure it not; for it is given unto the Gentiles: and the holy city shall they tread under foot forty and two months.

[3] And I will give power unto my two witnesses, and they shall prophesy a thousand two hundred and three-score days, clothed in sackcloth.

[4] These are the two olive trees, and the two candlesticks standing before the God of the earth.

[5] And if any man will hurt them, fire proceedeth out of their mouth, and devoureth their enemies: and if any man will hurt them, he must in this manner be killed.

[6] These have power to shut heaven, that it rain not in the days of their prophecy: and have power over waters to turn them to blood, and to smite the earth with all plagues, as often as they will.

[7] And when they shall have finished their testimony, the beast that ascendeth out of the bottomless pit shall make war against them, and shall overcome them, and kill them.

[8] And their dead bodies shall lie in the street of the great city, which spiritually is called Sodom and Egypt, where also our Lord was crucified.

[9] And they of the people and kindreds and tongues and nations shall see their dead bodies three days and an half, and shall not suffer their dead bodies to be put in graves.

[10] And they that dwell upon the earth shall rejoice over them, and make merry, and shall send gifts one to another; because these two prophets tormented them that dwelt on the earth.

[11] And after three days and an half the Spirit of life from God entered into them, and they stood upon their feet; and great fear fell upon them which saw them.

[12] And they heard a great voice from heaven saying unto them, Come up hither. And they ascended up to heaven in a cloud; and their enemies beheld them.

[13] And the same hour was there a great earthquake, and the tenth part of the city fell, and in the earthquake were slain of men seven thousand: and the remnant were affrighted, and gave glory to the God of heaven.

[14] The second woe is past; and, behold, the third woe cometh quickly.

[15] And the seventh angel sounded; and there were great voices in heaven, saying, The kingdoms of this world are become the kingdoms of our Lord, and of his Christ; and he shall reign for ever and ever.

[16] And the four and twenty elders, which sat before God on their seats, fell upon their faces, and worshipped God,

[17] Saying, We give thee thanks, O Lord God Almighty, which art, and wast, and art to come; because thou hast taken to thee thy great power, and hast reigned.

[18] And the nations were angry, and thy wrath is come, and the time of the dead, that they should be judged,

and that thou shouldest give reward unto thy servants the prophets, and to the saints, and them that fear thy name, small and great; and shouldest destroy them which destroy the earth.

[19] And the temple of God was opened in heaven, and there was seen in his temple the ark of his testament: and there were lightnings, and voices, and thunderings, and an earthquake, and great hail.

## Chapter 12

[1] And there appeared a great wonder in heaven; a woman clothed with the sun, and the moon under her feet, and upon her head a crown of twelve stars:

[2] And she being with child cried, travailing in birth, and pained to be delivered.

[3] And there appeared another wonder in heaven; and behold a great red dragon, having seven heads and ten horns, and seven crowns upon his heads.

[4] And his tail drew the third part of the stars of heaven, and did cast them to the earth: and the dragon stood before the woman which was ready to be delivered, for to devour her child as soon as it was born.

[5] And she brought forth a man child, who was to rule all nations with a rod of iron: and her child was caught up unto God, and to his throne.

[6] And the woman fled into the wilderness, where she hath a place prepared of God, that they should feed her there a thousand two hundred and threescore days.

[7] And there was war in heaven: Michael and his angels fought against the dragon; and the dragon fought and his angels,

[8] And prevailed not; neither was their place found any more in heaven.

[9] And the great dragon was cast out, that old serpent, called the Devil, and Satan, which deceiveth the whole world: he was cast out into the earth, and his angels were cast out with him.

[10] And I heard a loud voice saying in heaven, Now is come salvation, and strength, and the kingdom of our God, and the power of his Christ: for the accuser of our brethren is cast down, which accused them before our God day and night.

[11] And they overcame him by the blood of the Lamb, and by the word of their testimony; and they loved not their lives unto the death.

[12] Therefore rejoice, ye heavens, and ye that dwell in them. Woe to the inhabiters of the earth and of the sea! for the devil is come down unto you, having great wrath, because he knoweth that he hath but a short time.

[13] And when the dragon saw that he was cast unto the earth, he persecuted the woman which brought forth the man child.

[14] And to the woman were given two wings of a great eagle, that she might fly into the wilderness, into her place, where she is nourished for a time,

THE BOOK OF REVELATION—KJV

and times, and half a time, from the face of the serpent.

[15] And the serpent cast out of his mouth water as a flood after the woman, that he might cause her to be carried away of the flood.

[16] And the earth helped the woman, and the earth opened her mouth, and swallowed up the flood which the dragon cast out of his mouth.

[17] And the dragon was wroth with the woman, and went to make war with the remnant of her seed, which keep the commandments of God, and have the testimony of Jesus Christ.

## Chapter 13

[1] And I stood upon the sand of the sea, and saw a beast rise up out of the sea, having seven heads and ten horns, and upon his horns ten crowns, and upon his heads the name of blasphemy.

[2] And the beast which I saw was like unto a leopard, and his feet were as the feet of a bear, and his mouth as the mouth of a lion: and the dragon gave him his power, and his seat, and great authority.

[3] And I saw one of his heads as it were wounded to death; and his deadly wound was healed: and all the world wondered after the beast.

[4] And they worshipped the dragon which gave power unto the beast: and they worshipped the beast, saying, Who is like unto the beast? who is able to make war with him?

[5] And there was given unto him a mouth speaking great things and blasphemies; and power was given unto him to continue forty and two months.

[6] And he opened his mouth in blasphemy against God, to blaspheme his name, and his tabernacle, and them that dwell in heaven.

[7] And it was given unto him to make war with the saints, and to overcome them: and power was given him over all kindreds, and tongues, and nations.

[8] And all that dwell upon the earth shall worship him, whose names are not written in the book of life of the Lamb slain from the foundation of the world.

[9] If any man have an ear, let him hear.

[10] He that leadeth into captivity shall go into captivity: he that killeth with the sword must be killed with the sword. Here is the patience and the faith of the saints.

[11] And I beheld another beast coming up out of the earth; and he had two horns like a lamb, and he spake as a dragon.

[12] And he exerciseth all the power of the first beast before him, and causeth the earth and them which dwell therein to worship the first beast, whose deadly wound was healed.

[13] And he doeth great wonders, so that he maketh fire come down from heaven on the earth in the sight of men,

[14] And deceiveth them that dwell on the earth by the means of those miracles which he had power to do in the sight of the beast; saying to them that dwell on the earth, that they should make an image to the beast, which had the wound by a sword, and did live.

[15] And he had power to give life unto the image of the beast, that the image of the beast should both speak, and cause that as many as would not worship the image of the beast should be killed.

[16] And he causeth all, both small and great, rich and poor, free and bond, to receive a mark in their right hand, or in their foreheads:

[17] And that no man might buy or sell, save he that had the mark, or the name of the beast, or the number of his name.

[18] Here is wisdom. Let him that hath understanding count the number of the beast: for it is the number of a man; and his number is Six hundred threescore and six.

## Chapter 14

[1] And I looked, and, lo, a Lamb stood on the mount Sion, and with him an hundred forty and four thousand, having his Father's name written in their foreheads.

[2] And I heard a voice from heaven, as the voice of many waters, and as the voice of a great thunder: and I heard the voice of harpers harping with their harps:

[3] And they sung as it were a new song before the throne, and before the four beasts, and the elders: and no man could learn that song but the hundred and forty and four thousand, which were redeemed from the earth.

[4] These are they which were not defiled with women; for they are virgins. These are they which follow the Lamb whithersoever he goeth. These were redeemed from among men, being the firstfruits unto God and to the Lamb.

[5] And in their mouth was found no guile: for they are without fault before the throne of God.

[6] And I saw another angel fly in the midst of heaven, having the everlasting gospel to preach unto them that dwell on the earth, and to every nation, and kindred, and tongue, and people,

[7] Saying with a loud voice, Fear God, and give glory to him; for the hour of his judgment is come: and worship him that made heaven, and earth, and the sea, and the fountains of waters.

[8] And there followed another angel, saying, Babylon is fallen, is fallen, that great city, because she made all nations drink of the wine of the wrath of her fornication.

[9] And the third angel followed them, saying with a loud voice, If any man worship the beast and his image, and receive his mark in his forehead, or in his hand,

[10] The same shall drink of the wine of the wrath of God, which is poured out without mixture into the cup of

his indignation; and he shall be tormented with fire and brimstone in the presence of the holy angels, and in the presence of the Lamb:

[11] And the smoke of their torment ascendeth up for ever and ever: and they have no rest day nor night, who worship the beast and his image, and whosoever receiveth the mark of his name.

[12] Here is the patience of the saints: here are they that keep the commandments of God, and the faith of Jesus.

[13] And I heard a voice from heaven saying unto me, Write, Blessed are the dead which die in the Lord from henceforth: Yea, saith the Spirit, that they may rest from their labours; and their works do follow them.

[14] And I looked, and behold a white cloud, and upon the cloud one sat like unto the Son of man, having on his head a golden crown, and in his hand a sharp sickle.

[15] And another angel came out of the temple, crying with a loud voice to him that sat on the cloud, Thrust in thy sickle, and reap: for the time is come for thee to reap; for the harvest of the earth is ripe.

[16] And he that sat on the cloud thrust in his sickle on the earth; and the earth was reaped.

[17] And another angel came out of the temple which is in heaven, he also having a sharp sickle.

[18] And another angel came out from the altar, which had power over fire; and cried with a loud cry to him that had the sharp sickle, saying, Thrust in thy sharp sickle, and gather the clus-

ters of the vine of the earth; for her grapes are fully ripe.

[19] And the angel thrust in his sickle into the earth, and gathered the vine of the earth, and cast it into the great winepress of the wrath of God.

[20] And the winepress was trodden without the city, and blood came out of the winepress, even unto the horse bridles, by the space of a thousand and six hundred furlongs.

## Chapter 15

[1] And I saw another sign in heaven, great and marvellous, seven angels having the seven last plagues; for in them is filled up the wrath of God.

[2] And I saw as it were a sea of glass mingled with fire: and them that had gotten the victory over the beast, and over his image, and over his mark, and over the number of his name, stand on the sea of glass, having the harps of God.

[3] And they sing the song of Moses the servant of God, and the song of the Lamb, saying, Great and marvellous are thy works, Lord God Almighty; just and true are thy ways, thou King of saints.

[4] Who shall not fear thee, O Lord, and glorify thy name? for thou only art holy: for all nations shall come and worship before thee; for thy judgments are made manifest.

[5] And after that I looked, and, behold, the temple of the tabernacle of the testimony in heaven was opened:

[6] And the seven angels came out of the temple, having the seven plagues, clothed in pure and white linen, and having their breasts girded with golden girdles.

[7] And one of the four beasts gave unto the seven angels seven golden vials full of the wrath of God, who liveth for ever and ever.

[8] And the temple was filled with smoke from the glory of God, and from his power; and no man was able to enter into the temple, till the seven plagues of the seven angels were fulfilled.

## Chapter 16

[1] And I heard a great voice out of the temple saying to the seven angels, Go your ways, and pour out the vials of the wrath of God upon the earth.

[2] And the first went, and poured out his vial upon the earth; and there fell a noisome and grievous sore upon the men which had the mark of the beast, and upon them which worshipped his image.

[3] And the second angel poured out his vial upon the sea; and it became as the blood of a dead man: and every living soul died in the sea.

[4] And the third angel poured out his vial upon the rivers and fountains of waters; and they became blood.

[5] And I heard the angel of the waters say, Thou art righteous, O Lord, which art, and wast, and shalt be, because thou hast judged thus.

[6] For they have shed the blood of saints and prophets, and thou hast given them blood to drink; for they are worthy.

[7] And I heard another out of the altar say, Even so, Lord God Almighty, true and righteous are thy judgments.

[8] And the fourth angel poured out his vial upon the sun; and power was given unto him to scorch men with fire.

[9] And men were scorched with great heat, and blasphemed the name of God, which hath power over these plagues: and they repented not to give him glory.

[10] And the fifth angel poured out his vial upon the seat of the beast; and his kingdom was full of darkness; and they gnawed their tongues for pain,

[11] And blasphemed the God of heaven because of their pains and their sores, and repented not of their deeds.

[12] And the sixth angel poured out his vial upon the great river Euphrates; and the water thereof was dried up, that the way of the kings of the east might be prepared.

[13] And I saw three unclean spirits like frogs come out of the mouth of the dragon, and out of the mouth of the beast, and out of the mouth of the false prophet.

[14] For they are the spirits of devils, working miracles, which go forth unto the kings of the earth and of the whole world, to gather them to the battle of that great day of God Almighty.

THE BOOK OF REVELATION—KJV

[15] Behold, I come as a thief. Blessed is he that watcheth, and keepeth his garments, lest he walk naked, and they see his shame.

[16] And he gathered them together into a place called in the Hebrew tongue Armageddon.

[17] And the seventh angel poured out his vial into the air; and there came a great voice out of the temple of heaven, from the throne, saying, It is done.

[18] And there were voices, and thunders, and lightnings; and there was a great earthquake, such as was not since men were upon the earth, so mighty an earthquake, and so great.

[19] And the great city was divided into three parts, and the cities of the nations fell: and great Babylon came in remembrance before God, to give unto her the cup of the wine of the fierceness of his wrath.

[20] And every island fled away, and the mountains were not found.

[21] And there fell upon men a great hail out of heaven, every stone about the weight of a talent: and men blasphemed God because of the plague of the hail; for the plague thereof was exceeding great.

## Chapter 17

[1] And there came one of the seven angels which had the seven vials, and talked with me, saying unto me, Come hither; I will shew unto thee the judgment of the great whore that sitteth upon many waters:

[2] With whom the kings of the earth have committed fornication, and the inhabitants of the earth have been made drunk with the wine of her fornication.

[3] So he carried me away in the spirit into the wilderness: and I saw a woman sit upon a scarlet coloured beast, full of names of blasphemy, having seven heads and ten horns.

[4] And the woman was arrayed in purple and scarlet colour, and decked with gold and precious stones and pearls, having a golden cup in her hand full of abominations and filthiness of her fornication:

[5] And upon her forehead was a name written, MYSTERY, BABYLON THE GREAT, THE MOTHER OF HARLOTS AND ABOMINATIONS OF THE EARTH.

[6] And I saw the woman drunken with the blood of the saints, and with the blood of the martyrs of Jesus: and when I saw her, I wondered with great admiration.

[7] And the angel said unto me, Wherefore didst thou marvel? I will tell thee the mystery of the woman, and of the beast that carrieth her, which hath the seven heads and ten horns.

[8] The beast that thou sawest was, and is not; and shall ascend out of the bottomless pit, and go into perdition: and they that dwell on the earth shall wonder, whose names were not written in the book of life from the foundation of the world, when they behold the beast that was, and is not, and yet is.

[9] And here is the mind which hath wisdom. The seven heads are seven mountains, on which the woman sitteth.

[10] And there are seven kings: five are fallen, and one is, and the other is not yet come; and when he cometh, he must continue a short space.

[11] And the beast that was, and is not, even he is the eighth, and is of the seven, and goeth into perdition.

[12] And the ten horns which thou sawest are ten kings, which have received no kingdom as yet; but receive power as kings one hour with the beast.

[13] These have one mind, and shall give their power and strength unto the beast.

[14] These shall make war with the Lamb, and the Lamb shall overcome them: for he is Lord of lords, and King of kings: and they that are with him are called, and chosen, and faithful.

[15] And he saith unto me, The waters which thou sawest, where the whore sitteth, are peoples, and multitudes, and nations, and tongues.

[16] And the ten horns which thou sawest upon the beast, these shall hate the whore, and shall make her desolate and naked, and shall eat her flesh, and burn her with fire.

[17] For God hath put in their hearts to fulfill his will, and to agree, and give their kingdom unto the beast, until the words of God shall be fulfilled.

[18] And the woman which thou sawest is that great city, which reigneth over the kings of the earth.

## Chapter 18

[1] And after these things I saw another angel come down from heaven, having great power; and the earth was lightened with his glory.

[2] And he cried mightily with a strong voice, saying, Babylon the great is fallen, is fallen, and is become the habitation of devils, and the hold of every foul spirit, and a cage of every unclean and hateful bird.

[3] For all nations have drunk of the wine of the wrath of her fornication, and the kings of the earth have committed fornication with her, and the merchants of the earth are waxed rich through the abundance of her delicacies.

[4] And I heard another voice from heaven, saying, Come out of her, my people, that ye be not partakers of her sins, and that ye receive not of her plagues.

[5] For her sins have reached unto heaven, and God hath remembered her iniquities.

[6] Reward her even as she rewarded you, and double unto her double according to her works: in the cup which she hath filled fill to her double.

[7] How much she hath glorified herself, and lived deliciously, so much torment and sorrow give her: for she saith in her heart, I sit a queen, and am no widow, and shall see no sorrow.

[8] Therefore shall her plagues come in one day, death, and mourning, and famine; and she shall be utterly

burned with fire: for strong is the Lord God who judgeth her.

[9] And the kings of the earth, who have committed fornication and lived deliciously with her, shall bewail her, and lament for her, when they shall see the smoke of her burning,

[10] Standing afar off for the fear of her torment, saying, Alas, alas, that great city Babylon, that mighty city! for in one hour is thy judgment come.

[11] And the merchants of the earth shall weep and mourn over her; for no man buyeth their merchandise any more:

[12] The merchandise of gold, and silver, and precious stones, and of pearls, and fine linen, and purple, and silk, and scarlet, and all thyine wood, and all manner vessels of ivory, and all manner vessels of most precious wood, and of brass, and iron, and marble,

[13] And cinnamon, and odours, and ointments, and frankincense, and wine, and oil, and fine flour, and wheat, and beasts, and sheep, and horses, and chariots, and slaves, and souls of men.

[14] And the fruits that thy soul lusted after are departed from thee, and all things which were dainty and goodly are departed from thee, and thou shalt find them no more at all.

[15] The merchants of these things, which were made rich by her, shall stand afar off for the fear of her torment, weeping and wailing,

[16] And saying, Alas, alas, that great city, that was clothed in fine linen, and purple, and scarlet, and decked with gold, and precious stones, and pearls!

[17] For in one hour so great riches is come to nought. And every shipmaster, and all the company in ships, and sailors, and as many as trade by sea, stood afar off,

[18] And cried when they saw the smoke of her burning, saying, What city is like unto this great city!

[19] And they cast dust on their heads, and cried, weeping and wailing, saying, Alas, alas, that great city, wherein were made rich all that had ships in the sea by reason of her costliness! for in one hour is she made desolate.

[20] Rejoice over her, thou heaven, and ye holy apostles and prophets; for God hath avenged you on her.

[21] And a mighty angel took up a stone like a great millstone, and cast it into the sea, saying, Thus with violence shall that great city Babylon be thrown down, and shall be found no more at all.

[22] And the voice of harpers, and musicians, and of pipers, and trumpeters, shall be heard no more at all in thee; and no craftsman, of whatsoever craft he be, shall be found any more in thee; and the sound of a millstone shall be heard no more at all in thee;

[23] And the light of a candle shall shine no more at all in thee; and the voice of the bridegroom and of the bride shall be heard no more at all in thee: for thy merchants were the great men of the earth; for by thy sorceries were all nations deceived.

[24] And in her was found the blood of prophets, and of saints, and of all that were slain upon the earth.

## Chapter 19

[1] And after these things I heard a great voice of much people in heaven, saying, Alleluia; Salvation, and glory, and honour, and power, unto the Lord our God:

[2] For true and righteous are his judgments: for he hath judged the great whore, which did corrupt the earth with her fornication, and hath avenged the blood of his servants at her hand.

[3] And again they said, Alleluia. And her smoke rose up for ever and ever.

[4] And the four and twenty elders and the four beasts fell down and worshipped God that sat on the throne, saying, Amen; Alleluia.

[5] And a voice came out of the throne, saying, Praise our God, all ye his servants, and ye that fear him, both small and great.

[6] And I heard as it were the voice of a great multitude, and as the voice of many waters, and as the voice of mighty thunderings, saying, Alleluia: for the Lord God omnipotent reigneth.

[7] Let us be glad and rejoice, and give honour to him: for the marriage of the Lamb is come, and his wife hath made herself ready.

[8] And to her was granted that she should be arrayed in fine linen, clean and white: for the fine linen is the righteousness of saints.

[9] And he saith unto me, Write, Blessed are they which are called unto the marriage supper of the Lamb. And he saith unto me, These are the true sayings of God.

[10] And I fell at his feet to worship him. And he said unto me, See thou do it not: I am thy fellowservant, and of thy brethren that have the testimony of Jesus: worship God: for the testimony of Jesus is the spirit of prophecy.

[11] And I saw heaven opened, and behold a white horse; and he that sat upon him was called Faithful and True, and in righteousness he doth judge and make war.

[12] His eyes were as a flame of fire, and on his head were many crowns; and he had a name written, that no man knew, but he himself.

[13] And he was clothed with a vesture dipped in blood: and his name is called The Word of God.

[14] And the armies which were in heaven followed him upon white horses, clothed in fine linen, white and clean.

[15] And out of his mouth goeth a sharp sword, that with it he should smite the nations: and he shall rule them with a rod of iron: and he treadeth the winepress of the fierceness and wrath of Almighty God.

[16] And he hath on his vesture and on his thigh a name written, KING OF KINGS, AND LORD OF LORDS.

[17] And I saw an angel standing in the sun; and he cried with a loud voice, saying to all the fowls that fly in the midst of heaven, Come and gather

The Book of Revelation—KJV

yourselves together unto the supper of the great God;

[18] That ye may eat the flesh of kings, and the flesh of captains, and the flesh of mighty men, and the flesh of horses, and of them that sit on them, and the flesh of all men, both free and bond, both small and great.

[19] And I saw the beast, and the kings of the earth, and their armies, gathered together to make war against him that sat on the horse, and against his army.

[20] And the beast was taken, and with him the false prophet that wrought miracles before him, with which he deceived them that had received the mark of the beast, and them that worshipped his image. These both were cast alive into a lake of fire burning with brimstone.

[21] And the remnant were slain with the sword of him that sat upon the horse, which sword proceeded out of his mouth: and all the fowls were filled with their flesh.

## Chapter 20

[1] And I saw an angel come down from heaven, having the key of the bottomless pit and a great chain in his hand.

[2] And he laid hold on the dragon, that old serpent, which is the Devil, and Satan, and bound him a thousand years,

[3] And cast him into the bottomless pit, and shut him up, and set a seal upon him, that he should deceive the nations no more, till the thousand years should be fulfilled: and after that he must be loosed a little season.

[4] And I saw thrones, and they sat upon them, and judgment was given unto them: and I saw the souls of them that were beheaded for the witness of Jesus, and for the word of God, and which had not worshipped the beast, neither his image, neither had received his mark upon their foreheads, or in their hands; and they lived and reigned with Christ a thousand years.

[5] But the rest of the dead lived not again until the thousand years were finished. This is the first resurrection.

[6] Blessed and holy is he that hath part in the first resurrection: on such the second death hath no power, but they shall be priests of God and of Christ, and shall reign with him a thousand years.

[7] And when the thousand years are expired, Satan shall be loosed out of his prison,

[8] And shall go out to deceive the nations which are in the four quarters of the earth, Gog and Magog, to gather them together to battle: the number of whom is as the sand of the sea.

[9] And they went up on the breadth of the earth, and compassed the camp of the saints about, and the beloved city: and fire came down from God out of heaven, and devoured them.

[10] And the devil that deceived them was cast into the lake of fire and brimstone, where the beast and the false prophet are, and shall be tormented day and night for ever and ever.

[11] And I saw a great white throne, and him that sat on it, from whose face the earth and the heaven fled away; and there was found no place for them.

[12] And I saw the dead, small and great, stand before God; and the books were opened: and another book was opened, which is the book of life: and the dead were judged out of those things which were written in the books, according to their works.

[13] And the sea gave up the dead which were in it; and death and hell delivered up the dead which were in them: and they were judged every man according to their works.

[14] And death and hell were cast into the lake of fire. This is the second death.

[15] And whosoever was not found written in the book of life was cast into the lake of fire.

### Chapter 21

[1] And I saw a new heaven and a new earth: for the first heaven and the first earth were passed away; and there was no more sea.

[2] And I John saw the holy city, new Jerusalem, coming down from God out of heaven, prepared as a bride adorned for her husband.

[3] And I heard a great voice out of heaven saying, Behold, the tabernacle of God is with men, and he will dwell with them, and they shall be his people, and God himself shall be with them, and be their God.

[4] And God shall wipe away all tears from their eyes; and there shall be no more death, neither sorrow, nor crying, neither shall there be any more pain: for the former things are passed away.

[5] And he that sat upon the throne said, Behold, I make all things new. And he said unto me, Write: for these words are true and faithful.

[6] And he said unto me, It is done. I am Alpha and Omega, the beginning and the end. I will give unto him that is athirst of the fountain of the water of life freely.

[7] He that overcometh shall inherit all things; and I will be his God, and he shall be my son.

[8] But the fearful, and unbelieving, and the abominable, and murderers, and whoremongers, and sorcerers, and idolaters, and all liars, shall have their part in the lake which burneth with fire and brimstone: which is the second death.

[9] And there came unto me one of the seven angels which had the seven vials full of the seven last plagues, and talked with me, saying, Come hither, I will shew thee the bride, the Lamb's wife.

[10] And he carried me away in the spirit to a great and high mountain, and shewed me that great city, the holy Jerusalem, descending out of heaven from God,

[11] Having the glory of God: and her light was like unto a stone most precious, even like a jasper stone, clear as crystal;

THE BOOK OF REVELATION—KJV

[12] And had a wall great and high, and had twelve gates, and at the gates twelve angels, and names written thereon, which are the names of the twelve tribes of the children of Israel:

[13] On the east three gates; on the north three gates; on the south three gates; and on the west three gates.

[14] And the wall of the city had twelve foundations, and in them the names of the twelve apostles of the Lamb.

[15] And he that talked with me had a golden reed to measure the city, and the gates thereof, and the wall thereof.

[16] And the city lieth foursquare, and the length is as large as the breadth: and he measured the city with the reed, twelve thousand furlongs. The length and the breadth and the height of it are equal.

[17] And he measured the wall thereof, an hundred and forty and four cubits, according to the measure of a man, that is, of the angel.

[18] And the building of the wall of it was of jasper: and the city was pure gold, like unto clear glass.

[19] And the foundations of the wall of the city were garnished with all manner of precious stones. The first foundation was jasper; the second, sapphire; the third, a chalcedony; the fourth, an emerald;

[20] The fifth, sardonyx; the sixth, sardius; the seventh, chrysolite; the eighth, beryl; the ninth, a topaz; the tenth, a chrysoprasus; the eleventh, a jacinth; the twelfth, an amethyst.

[21] And the twelve gates were twelve pearls; every several gate was of one pearl: and the street of the city was pure gold, as it were transparent glass.

[22] And I saw no temple therein: for the Lord God Almighty and the Lamb are the temple of it.

[23] And the city had no need of the sun, neither of the moon, to shine in it: for the glory of God did lighten it, and the Lamb is the light thereof.

[24] And the nations of them which are saved shall walk in the light of it: and the kings of the earth do bring their glory and honour into it.

[25] And the gates of it shall not be shut at all by day: for there shall be no night there.

[26] And they shall bring the glory and honour of the nations into it.

[27] And there shall in no wise enter into it any thing that defileth, neither whatsoever worketh abomination, or maketh a lie: but they which are written in the Lamb's book of life.

## Chapter 22

[1] And he shewed me a pure river of water of life, clear as crystal, proceeding out of the throne of God and of the Lamb.

[2] In the midst of the street of it, and on either side of the river, was there the tree of life, which bare twelve manner of fruits, and yielded her fruit every month: and the leaves of the tree were for the healing of the nations.

[3] And there shall be no more curse: but the throne of God and of the Lamb shall be in it; and his servants shall serve him:

[4] And they shall see his face; and his name shall be in their foreheads.

[5] And there shall be no night there; and they need no candle, neither light of the sun; for the Lord God giveth them light: and they shall reign for ever and ever.

[6] And he said unto me, These sayings are faithful and true: and the Lord God of the holy prophets sent his angel to shew unto his servants the things which must shortly be done.

[7] Behold, I come quickly: blessed is he that keepeth the sayings of the prophecy of this book.

[8] And I John saw these things, and heard them. And when I had heard and seen, I fell down to worship before the feet of the angel which shewed me these things.

[9] Then saith he unto me, See thou do it not: for I am thy fellowservant, and of thy brethren the prophets, and of them which keep the sayings of this book: worship God.

[10] And he saith unto me, Seal not the sayings of the prophecy of this book: for the time is at hand.

[11] He that is unjust, let him be unjust still: and he which is filthy, let him be filthy still: and he that is righteous, let him be righteous still: and he that is holy, let him be holy still.

[12] And, behold, I come quickly; and my reward is with me, to give every man according as his work shall be.

[13] I am Alpha and Omega, the beginning and the end, the first and the last.

[14] Blessed are they that do his commandments, that they may have right to the tree of life, and may enter in through the gates into the city.

[15] For without are dogs, and sorcerers, and whoremongers, and murderers, and idolaters, and whosoever loveth and maketh a lie.

[16] I Jesus have sent mine angel to testify unto you these things in the churches. I am the root and the offspring of David, and the bright and morning star.

[17] And the Spirit and the bride say, Come. And let him that heareth say, Come. And let him that is athirst come. And whosoever will, let him take the water of life freely.

[18] For I testify unto every man that heareth the words of the prophecy of this book, If any man shall add unto these things, God shall add unto him the plagues that are written in this book:

[19] And if any man shall take away from the words of the book of this prophecy, God shall take away his part out of the book of life, and out of the holy city, and from the things which are written in this book.

[20] He which testifieth these things saith, Surely I come quickly. Amen. Even so, come, Lord Jesus.

[21] The grace of our Lord Jesus Christ be with you all. Amen.

THE BOOK OF REVELATION—KJV

# REVELATION

**1** [1] This book is what Jesus Christ revealed. God gave this revelation to Jesus to show his servants the things which must happen soon. Jesus revealed it to John, his servant, sending it through his angel. [2] John told the truth about the things he saw—the testimony of Jesus Christ and the message of God. [3] Happy is the person who reads the words of this prophecy, listens to them, and obeys the things written here, because the time is near.

## Seven Congregations

[4] From John.

To the seven congregations in the land of Asia.[a]

The One who is, who was, and who will be *sends* you gracious love and peace; so do the seven spirits who are before God's throne. [5-6] Gracious love and peace from Jesus Christ, too. He is the faithful Witness, the first one to rise from death, and the Ruler of the kings of earth.

May glory and power be his forever and ever. Amen! Jesus loved us. He bled, setting us free from our sins. He formed us into a kingdom. We are priests to God, his Father.

> *"I am the A and the Z"* says the Lord God. He is the One who is, who was, and who will be. He is all-powerful.
>
> *Revelation 1:8*

[7] "Look! He is coming with the clouds." *Daniel 7:13*
"Every eye will see him;
    even those who wounded him." *Zechariah 12:10,12,14*
Because of him, all people on earth will cry.
Yes, amen!

[8] "I am the A and the Z"[b] says the Lord God. He is the One who is, who was, and who will be. He is all-powerful.

## John on Patmos

[9] I am John, your brother. In Jesus I share with you the trouble, the endurance, and the kingdom. I was on an island called Patmos. *They put*

---

1:4   [a]   modern Turkey
1:8   [b]   literally, the Alpha and the Omega (the first and the last letters of the Greek alphabet). Here it means the beginning and the end.

191

*me there*, because *I proclaimed* the message of God and the evidence about Jesus. [10] During the Lord's day, I was in the Spirit. I heard a loud voice *speaking* behind me. It was like the sound from a trumpet. [11] It said, "Write what you see in a scroll. Send it to these seven congregations: Ephesus, Smyrna, Pergamum, Thyatira, Sardis, Philadelphia, Laodicea."

> *I am the one who is alive. I was dead, but, look, I am alive forever and ever!*
> *Revelation 1:18*

[12] I turned around to look at the voice which was talking to me. After I turned around, I saw seven golden lampstands. [13] There was one like the Son of Man[c] among them. He was dressed with a very long robe. He wore a golden belt around his waist. [14] His head and his hair were white, white like wool or like snow. His eyes were like the flame of a fire. [15] His feet were like brass, glowing in an oven. His voice was loud, like *the rushing of* much water. [16] He had seven stars in his right hand. A sword, sharp on both edges, was coming out of his mouth. His face looked like the sun, when it shines its brightest.

[17] When I saw him, I fell down at his feet as if I were dead. Then he put his right hand on me and said, "Don't be afraid! I am the first and the last. [18] I am the one who is alive. I was dead, but, look, I am alive forever and ever! I have the keys to death and Hades.[d] [19] So write the things which you saw, the things that are now and the things that are about to happen after the present time. [20] This is the secret of the seven stars in my right hand and the seven golden lampstands which you saw on my right: The seven stars are the messengers of the seven congregations. The seven lampstands are the seven congregations."

## Ephesus

2 [1] "Write this to the messenger of the congregation in Ephesus: The one who is holding the seven stars in his right hand, the one who is walking among the seven golden lampstands, says this: [2] 'I know what you have done, how hard you have worked, and how patient you have been. I know that you cannot tolerate evil people. You have tested those men who call themselves apostles. They are not apostles. You found out that they are liars! [3] You have endurance. Yet you have carried on because of my name; you've not become tired. [4] But I have something against you—you

---

1:13  [c] See Daniel 7:13-14. This refers to Jesus, the Messiah.
1:18  [d] the Greek word for the unseen world of the dead

no longer love me as you did in the beginning. [5] Therefore, remember from where you have fallen. Change your heart! Do the things you did in the beginning. If you won't change your heart, I will come and take your lampstand from its place. [6] However, you **do** have this—you hate what the Nicolaitan people[a] are doing. I hate those things, too. [7] The person who has an ear should listen to what the Spirit is saying to the congregations. To the person who conquers I will give something to eat. It will come from the Tree of Life, which is in the Paradise[b] of God.' "

## Smyrna

[8] "Write this to the messenger of the congregation in Smyrna: The one who is the first and the last, who was dead and came back to life, says this: [9] 'I know your troubles and how poor you are (but you are actually rich) and I know about the slander of those who call themselves Jews. (They are not Jews; they are a synagogue of Satan!) [10] Don't be afraid of anything you are about to suffer. Look, the Devil is about to throw some of you into prison. He wants to test you. You will have trouble for ten days. Be faithful, even if you must die. I will give you the crown[c] of life. [11] The person who has an ear should listen to what the Spirit is saying to the congregations. The person who conquers will never be hurt by the second death.' "

## Pergamum

[12] "Write this to the messenger of the congregation in Pergamum: The one who has the sword which is sharp on both edges says, [13] 'I know where you live (It is Satan's throne.), but you are holding onto my name. You did not leave my faith, even during the time of Antipas, my faithful witness. He was taken from you and killed. Satan lives where you are. [14] But I have a few things against you: You have some people there who are holding onto Balaam's teaching.[d] Balaam was teaching Balak to put a temptation in front of the sons of Israel to make them sin, to eat food offered to false gods and to make them commit sexual sin. [15] In the same way, you have some people there who are also holding onto the teaching of the Nicolaitans. [16] So, change your hearts! If you don't, I will come soon. I will make war against them with the sword which comes from my mouth. [17] The person who has an ear should listen to what the Spirit is saying to

---

2:6   [a]   followers of Nicolas. It may be the same person in Acts 6:5.
2:7   [b]   See Genesis 2:8-17.
2:10  [c]   reward
2:14  [d]   See Numbers 22—24; Deuteronomy 23:3-4.

the congregations. I will give some of the hidden manna[e] to the person who conquers. I will also give him a little white stone. A new name[f] will have been written on the stone. The only person who knows the name is the one who gets it.' "

## Thyatira

[18] "Write this to the messenger of the congregation in Thyatira: The Son of God, whose eyes are like the flame of a fire and whose feet are like shining brass, says, [19] 'I know your deeds, your love, your faith, your service, and your endurance. You are doing more now than you did in the beginning. [20] However, I have something against you: You are tolerating that woman, Jezebel.[g] She calls herself a prophetess. She fools my servants and teaches them to commit sexual sin and to eat food offered to false gods. [21] I gave her time to change her heart, but she didn't want to stop committing sexual sin. [22] Look! If she and the men who are committing adultery with her are not sorry for what they have done, I will throw them on a bed of great trouble. [23] I will kill her children.[h] Then all of the congregations will know that I am the one who searches the deepest human thoughts and feelings. The way you live is the way I will reward each one of you. [24] Some of you in Thyatira do not hold to this teaching. You don't know "the deep things of Satan." I am not putting another burden upon you. [25] Hold onto what you have until I come. [26] I will give authority over the people of the world to the person who conquers and always obeys me. [27-28] I have received this *authority* from my Father. He will take care of His enemies like a shepherd does—with an iron rod, shattering them like clay pots.[i] I will also give him the Morning Star.[j] [29] The person who has an ear should listen to what the Spirit is saying to the congregations.' "

## Sardis

3 [1] "Write this to the messenger of the congregation in Sardis: The one who has the seven spirits of God and the seven stars says this: 'I know what you have done. People may think you are alive, but you are dead! [2] Wake up! Make strong the things which remain and are about to die. I have not found your actions complete before my God. [3] So, remember what you have received and heard. Then obey it. Change your

---

2:17   [e] Perhaps this is explained by John 6:31-36.
2:17   [f] Compare Exodus 28:36-38; 1 Peter 2:9; Revelation 14:1.
2:20   [g] A vengeful, merciless, pagan queen. See 1 Kings 16:31–21:23; 2 Kings 9:7,30-37
2:23   [h] This probably refers to her followers.
2:27-28   [i] Clay pots are very brittle; they cannot stand against iron which is very hard and strong.
2:27-28   [j] Jesus. See Revelation 22:16.

heart! If you don't wake up, I will come like a robber. You will never know precisely when I will come upon you. [4] However, you have a few individuals in Sardis who have not polluted their clothes.[a] They will walk with me *dressed* in white;[b] they are worthy people. [5] In the same way, the person who conquers will wear white clothes. His name will never be erased from the Book of Life. I will speak for him in front of my Father and in front of His angels. [6] The person who has an ear should listen to what the Spirit is saying to the congregations.' "

## Philadelphia

[7] "Write this to the messenger of the congregation in Philadelphia: The one who is holy and true says, 'He has David's key. He opens, and no one closes; he closes, and no one opens. [8] I know what you have done. Listen! I have put a door in front of you. It is open. No one can close it. Though you don't have much strength, you have obeyed my teaching and have not denied my name. [9] Look, I will handle those from the synagogue of Satan. They call themselves true Jews, but they are not. They are lying. Listen! I will make them come and bow down at your feet. Then they will know that I have loved you. [10] You obeyed my teaching about endurance. Now, I will keep you from the time of testing which is about to come upon the whole world. All people on earth will be tested. [11] I am coming soon. Hold onto what you have, so that no one can take away your crown.[c] [12] I will make the victorious person a pillar in the temple sanctuary of my God. He will never leave there. On him I will write my new name, my God's name, and the name of the city of my God. That city is the new Jerusalem, which is coming down from heaven from my God. [13] The person who has an ear should listen to what the Spirit is saying to the congregations.' "

> *I have put a door in front of you. It is open. No one can close it.*
> *Revelation 3:8*

## Laodicea

[14] "Write this to the messenger of the congregation in Laodicea: The Amen, the faithful and true Witness, the Source of God's creation says: [15] 'I know what you've done. You are not cold; you are not hot. I wish you were either cold or hot! [16] Instead, you are lukewarm—not hot, not cold. So, I am going to vomit you out of my mouth. [17] You say, "I am rich." You

---

3:4 [a] They have lived good lives. See 1 Corinthians 6:11.
3:4 [b] White symbolizes purity.
3:11 [c] reward

> *I will make the victorious person a pillar in the temple sanctuary of my God. He will never leave there.*
>
> *Revelation 3:12*

*think* you have been rich and you don't need anything. Don't you realize that you are miserable, pitiful, poor, blind, and naked? [18] I advise you to buy refined gold from me, so that you may truly be rich. Buy white clothes from me, so that you will be dressed and you won't see the shame of your nakedness. Buy medicine from me to rub into your eyes, so that you may see. [19] I correct and punish those whom I love. Be serious. Change your heart! [20] Listen, I stand at the door. I am knocking. If anyone hears my voice and opens the door, I will come inside with him. We will have dinner together. [21] I will give *the right* to sit with me at my throne to the person who conquers as I conquered, and as I sat down beside my Father at His throne. [22] The person who has an ear should listen to what the Spirit is saying to the congregations.' "

## The Throne

4 [1] Later I looked and there was an open door in heaven. The voice which I had heard before was talking to me. It sounded *loud*, like a trumpet: "Come up here! I will show you things which must happen later." [2] Immediately, I was in the Spirit. Look, a throne was put there in heaven. One was sitting on it. [3] He looked like jasper and carnelian—precious jewels. There was a rainbow around the throne. It looked like an emerald. [4] There were twenty-four thrones around the throne and twenty-four elders were sitting on the thrones. They were dressed in white clothes.[a] They had golden crowns on their heads, too. [5] Lightning, thunder, and rumblings came from the throne. Seven lamps were burning in front of the throne. (They are the seven spirits of God.) [6] In front of the throne there was something like a glass lake; it looked like crystal.

There were four beings next to the throne and all around it. They had eyes everywhere—in front and behind. [7] The first being was like a lion. The second being was like a bull. The third being had a face like a man's face. And the fourth being was like an eagle flying. [8] Each of the four beings had six wings and each one was covered with eyes—inside and outside. Day and night they never stopped saying this:

"Holy, holy, holy is the Lord God,
   the all-powerful One;
      the One who was, who is, and who will be."

---

4:4   [a] White symbolizes purity.

[9] The four beings give glory, honor, and thanks to the One who is sitting on the throne and who lives forever and ever. [10] Then the twenty-four elders fall down in front of the One who is sitting on the throne. They worship the One who lives forever and ever. They lay their crowns before the throne, saying:

[11] "O Lord, our God, You are worthy
to receive glory, honor, and power,
because You made everything.
All things were created because of Your will."

## Who Is Worthy?

5 [1] I saw a scroll[a] on the right of the One who was sitting on the throne. The scroll had writing on both sides of it. It was sealed with seven seals. [2] And I saw a strong angel. He was announcing this loudly: "Who is worthy to open the scroll, to open its seals?" [3] But there was no one in heaven, on earth, or under the earth who could open the scroll. No one could look inside it. [4] I was in tears, because no one could be found. No one was worthy to open the scroll. No one could look inside it.

[5] One of the elders said to me, "Don't cry! Look, the Lion from the tribe of Judah has been victorious. He is the Descendant[b] of David. He will open the scroll and its seven seals."

[6] Then I saw a Lamb standing there. It looked as though it had been killed. It was very close to the throne and the four beings, surrounded by the elders. It had seven horns and seven eyes.

> *Listen, I stand at the door. I am knocking.*
> Revelation 3:20

(These are the seven spirits of God sent to the whole earth.) [7] It came and took the scroll from the right hand of the One who was sitting on the throne. [8] When it did this, the four beings and the twenty-four elders fell down in front of the Lamb. They had harps and golden bowls full of incense.[c] (These are the prayers of the holy people.) [9] They sang a new song:

"You are worthy to take the scroll
and to open its seals,
because you were killed; you used your blood
to buy back some people for God

---

5:1 [a] a long roll of leather or papyrus used for writing on a book
5:5 [b] Jesus
5:8 [c] A special powder used in Jewish worship (Luke 1:9). It smelled good when it was burned. Compare Numbers 16:46-47; Psalm 141:2.

from every tribe, language, people, and nation.

[10] You changed them into a kingdom and priests for our God.

They will rule over the earth."

[11] I looked, and I heard the sound of many angels, the four beings, and the elders around the throne. The number of them was thousands of thousands and ten thousands of ten thousands. [12] They shouted:

"The Lamb who was killed is worthy to receive

power, wealth, wisdom, strength, honor, glory, and

praise!"

[13] And I heard every creature in heaven, on earth, under the earth, and in the ocean, and everything that is in them. They said this:

"Praise, honor, glory, and power belong to the One

who is sitting on the throne and to the Lamb

forever and ever."

[14] The four beings said again and again, "Amen!" And the elders fell down and worshiped.

## The Seven Seals

6 [1] I watched as the Lamb opened one of the seven seals. Then I heard one of the four beings say with a voice as loud as thunder, "Come!" [2] I looked, and there was a white horse. The person riding it had a bow. He was given a crown. As a conquerer, he rode out to conquer.

[3] And when the Lamb opened the second seal, I heard the second being say, "Come!" [4] And another horse came out. It was red like fire. The person riding it was told to take peace away from the people of the earth, so that they would kill one another. He was given a great sword.

[5] And when the Lamb opened the third seal, I heard the third being say, "Come!" I looked, and there was a black horse. The person who was riding it had weighing scales[a] in his hand. [6] I heard something like a voice come from among the four beings. It said, "A quart of wheat for a silver coin,[b] three quarts of barley for a silver coin, but don't hurt the olive oil or the wine."

[7] And when the Lamb opened the fourth seal, I heard the voice of the fourth being say, "Come!" [8] I looked and there was a pale-colored horse. The rider was named Death. Hades[c] was following him. They were given

---

6:5   [a]   Bread was sold by weight. This shows how precious even a little food was.

6:6   [b]   Normally, a silver coin would buy eight to twelve times more. Inflation hurts poor people much more than the rich.

6:8   [c]   the Greek word for the unseen world of the dead

authority over one-fourth of the earth. They could kill with the sword, with famine, with disease, or use wild animals from the earth.

⁹ And when the Lamb opened the fifth seal, I saw under the altar the souls of those who had been killed because *they had preached* the message of God and because of the testimony that they had *given*. ¹⁰ They pleaded loudly, "How long, holy and true Master? Will you ever judge the people on earth and pay them back for killing us?"

¹¹ Each of them was given a white robe. They were told to rest a little while longer, until everything was complete. (Their co-slaves and their brothers were also about to be killed, as they had been killed.)

¹² And when the Lamb had opened the sixth seal, I observed a great earthquake. The sun became black like sackcloth made of goat hair. The whole moon became *red* like blood. ¹³ The stars of the sky fell to earth, as a fig tree drops its figs when it is shaken by a strong wind. ¹⁴ The sky disappeared like a scroll which is rolled up. Every mountain and island was moved from its place. ¹⁵ The kings of the earth, the important men, commanders, rich men, strong men, all slaves and free men hid themselves in caves and among the rocks of the mountains. ¹⁶ And they said to the mountains and to the rocks, "Fall on us. Hide us from the face of the One who is sitting on the throne. Hide us from the Lamb's punishment." ¹⁷ The great Day of his anger has come. Who will be able to stand?

## The 144,000

7 ¹ Later I saw four angels standing at the four corners of the earth. They were holding back the four winds of the earth, so that no wind could blow upon the earth, upon the ocean, or upon any tree. ² I saw another angel coming up from the east. He had the seal of the living God. He shouted to the four angels who were told to hurt the earth and the ocean, ³ "Don't hurt the earth, the ocean, or the trees until we put a seal on the foreheads of the servants of our God." ⁴ I heard the number of those who had been sealed. It was 144,000 from every tribe of the sons of Israel:[a]

⁵ 12,000 sealed from the tribe of Judah,
12,000 sealed from the tribe of Reuben,
12,000 sealed from the tribe of Gad,
⁶ 12,000 sealed from the tribe of Asher,
12,000 sealed from the tribe of Naphtali,
12,000 sealed from the tribe of Manasseh,
⁷ 12,000 sealed from the tribe of Simeon,

---

7:4    [a] Twelve was a complete number to the Jews. 12,000 x 12 symbolized all of God's people.

12,000 sealed from the tribe of Levi,
12,000 sealed from the tribe of Issachar,
[8] 12,000 sealed from the tribe of Zebulun,
12,000 sealed from the tribe of Joseph,
12,000 sealed from the tribe of Benjamin.

## A Large Crowd of People

[9] Later I looked and there was such a large crowd of people that no one could count them. They came from every nation, tribe, people, and language. They were standing in front of the throne and in front of the Lamb. They were dressed in white robes. Palm branches were in their hands. [10] They shouted, "Salvation belongs to our God, the One who is sitting on the throne! Salvation belongs to the Lamb, too!"

[11] All the angels stood around the elders and the four beings, around the throne. They fell down on their faces in front of the throne and worshiped God. [12] They said, "Amen! Praise, glory, wisdom, thanks, honor, power, and strength belong to our God forever and ever! Amen!"

[13] One of the elders asked me, "Who are those people dressed in white robes? Where did they come from?"

[14] I answered him, "Sir, **you** know!"

He said to me, "They are the ones who came through the great trouble *safely*. Using the Lamb's blood, they washed their robes to make them white. [15] This is why they are before God's throne. They worship God day and night in His temple sanctuary. The One who is sitting on the throne will live with them. [16] They will never be hungry or thirsty. No heat or sun will burn them. [17] The Lamb in the middle of the throne will take care of them, like a shepherd does.[b] He will lead them to springs of fresh[c] water. God will wipe away every tear from their eyes."[d]

## Silence in Heaven

8 [1] And when the Lamb opened the seventh seal, there was silence in heaven for about half an hour. [2] I saw seven angels, who always stand in front of God. They were given seven trumpets.

[3] Another angel came and stood at the golden altar. He had a golden censer.[a] He was given much incense,[b] so that he could offer it with all the holy people's prayers on the altar before the throne. [4] The smoke from the

---

7:17   [b]  See Psalm 23:1; Ezekiel 34:23; John 10:11,14.
7:17   [c]  literally, living
7:17   [d]  See Isaiah 25:8; Revelation 21:4.
8:3    [a]  a container in which incense was burned
8:3    [b]  A special powder used in Jewish worship (Luke 1:9). It smelled good when it was burned. Compare Numbers 16:46-47; Psalm 141:2.

incense went up from the angel's hand before God, with the prayers of the holy people. [5] The angel took the censer and filled it with fire from the altar. Then he threw it on the earth. Thunder, rumblings, lightning, and an earthquake took place.

## The Seven Trumpets

[6] The seven angels who had the seven trumpets prepared to sound them.

[7] The first angel sounded his trumpet. There was hail and fire, mixed with blood. This was thrown on the earth. One-third of the earth was burned up. One-third of the trees were burned up. And, all of the green grass was burned up.

[8] The second angel sounded his trumpet. Something like a great burning mountain was thrown into the ocean. One-third of the ocean was changed into blood. [9] One-third of the living creatures in the ocean died. One-third of the ships were destroyed.

[10] The third angel sounded his trumpet. A great star fell from the sky. It was burning like a torch. It fell on one-third of the rivers and on the springs of water. [11] The name of that star is Bitterness.[c] It changed one-third of the water into bitter water. Many people died because of the water; it was poison.

[12] The fourth angel sounded his trumpet. He struck one-third of the sun, one-third of the moon, and one-third of the stars. One-third of them became dark. The day was only one-third as bright as usual. And the night was two-thirds darker.

[13] I looked and I heard an eagle flying in the middle of the air. It was shouting, "How horrible! How horrible! How horrible it will be for people who live on earth! There will be three more such blasts of trumpets in the future by three more angels."

9 [1] The fifth angel sounded his trumpet. I saw a star which had fallen to the ground from the sky. He was given the key to the bottomless pit. [2] He opened it. Smoke came up from the pit like the smoke from a great oven. The smoke from the pit made the sun and the air dark. [3] Grasshoppers came from the smoke and went into the world. They were given power, like that of scorpions on earth. [4] They were told not to hurt the grass of the earth, any green plant, or any tree. They could only hurt those who did not have God's seal on their foreheads. [5] They were not allowed to kill them—only to torture them for five months. The pain they suffered was like that of a scorpion when it stings someone. [6] During that

---

8:11    [c]  literally, Wormwood

time, people will look for death, but they won't find it. They will want to die, but death will run away from them.

[7] The grasshoppers looked like horses prepared for war. They had crowns like gold on their heads. Their faces looked like the faces of people. [8] They had hair like the hair of women. Their teeth were like lion's teeth. [9] They had chests like iron breastplates. The sound of their wings was like the roar of many horses and chariots running into battle. [10] Their tails were like scorpions' tails. They had stingers in them, with the power to hurt human beings for five months. [11] They had a king over them. He was an angel from the bottomless *pit*. In Hebrew his name is Abaddon.[a] In Greek it is Apollyon.[b]

[12] One horror has gone. But listen, there are still two more to come!

[13] The sixth angel sounded his trumpet. I heard a sound coming from the corners[c] of the golden altar, which is in front of God. [14] It said to the sixth angel with the trumpet, "You must release the four angels! They have been bound at the great river Euphrates." [15] So the four angels were released. They had been prepared for this *exact* hour of this *exact* day of this *exact* month of this *exact* year to kill one-third of mankind. [16] The number of soldiers on horses was 200 million (I overheard the number.). [17] In the same way, in my vision I saw the horses and their riders. They had fiery red, yellow, and blue armor. The heads of the horses were like the heads of lions. Fire, smoke, and sulfur came out of their mouths. [18] One-third of mankind was killed by these three plagues—the fire, the smoke, and the sulfur that came from their mouths. [19] The power of the horses was in their mouths and in their tails. Their tails had heads on them like snakes. They could use them to hurt people.

[20] Some people were not killed by these plagues. They did not change their hearts about the things they had made with their hands—false gods made of gold, silver, brass, stone, and wood—things which cannot see, hear, or walk. These people did not stop worshiping demons. [21] They were not sorry about their murders, their evil magic, the sexual sin they had committed, or their robberies.

## A Strong Angel

10 [1] Then I saw another strong angel coming down from heaven. He was dressed with a cloud. A rainbow was above his head. His face was *shining* like the sun, and his legs were like columns of fire.

---

9:11    [a] a Hebrew name meaning "destruction"

9:11    [b] a Greek name meaning "destruction"

9:13    [c] Blood was often placed on the corners (horns) of the incense altar (Leviticus 4:7). Compare Revelation 8:3-5.

²He had a little scroll in his hand; it was not rolled up. He put his right foot in the ocean and his left foot on land. ³He shouted very loudly, like when a lion roars. After he shouted, the seven thunders *answered* with rumblings. ⁴After the seven thunders spoke, I was just about to write this down. But I heard a voice from heaven say, "Seal up what the seven thunders said. Don't write those things!"

⁵The angel that I saw standing in the ocean and on land raised his right hand to heaven. ⁶He vowed by the One who lives forever and ever, by God who made heaven and everything in it, the earth and everything on it, and the ocean and everything in it. He said, "There will be no more time!"

⁷But, during the time when the seventh angel is about to sound his trumpet, God's secret plan will be finished, just as He announced to His servants, the prophets.

⁸The voice that I had heard from heaven was speaking to me again. It said, "Go, take the scroll which is unrolled in the angel's hand. He is standing in the ocean and on land."

⁹I went to the angel and asked him to give me the scroll. He said to me, "Take it and eat it! It will be sweet as honey in your mouth, but it will be sour in your stomach." ¹⁰So, I took the little scroll from the angel's hand and ate it. And it tasted as sweet as honey in my mouth, but when I ate it, it made my stomach sour. ¹¹Then they said to me, "You must prophesy again to the peoples, nations, languages, and to many kings."

## Two Prophets of God

**11** ¹I was given a long measuring stick. It was like a rod. He said, "Get up! Measure God's temple sanctuary and the altar, and count the people who are worshiping there. ²But don't measure the court outside the temple sanctuary, because it is for non-Jews.ᵃ They will trample the holy city for 42 months. ³I will give my two witnesses *power*. They will prophesy for 1,260 days, while they are dressed in sackcloth.ᵇ ⁴(These men are the two olive trees and the two lampstands that stand before the Lord of the earth.) ⁵If any enemy wants to hurt them, a fire comes out of their mouth and burns them up. Any person who tries to hurt them will die like this. ⁶They have the authority to shut the sky. It won't rain while they are prophesying. They also have the authority to change all water into blood. They can strike the earth with any plague as often as they wish. ⁷When they finish giving their evidence, the wild animal that comes up from the bottomless *pit* will fight them and he will defeat them.

11:2 ᵃ or, the nations
11:3 ᵇ This was a very rough kind of cloth. It was worn by people who mourned a death or who felt very sorry or sad about some other serious trouble. Compare Matthew 11:21.

He will kill them. [8-9] Their dead bodies *will lie exposed* in the streets of the great city. (Spiritually, it is named Sodom and Egypt, where their Lord was nailed to the cross.) They won't allow their bodies to be buried. People from every nation, tribe, language, and race will look at the bodies for three and a half days. [10] The people who live on earth will be very happy. They will have a party. They will exchange gifts, because the two prophets *died*. They had made the people who live on earth suffer. [11] But, after the three and a half days, the breath of life[c] from God will come[d] into them. They will stand up. The people who will be watching them will become very afraid. [12] Then the two prophets will hear a loud voice speaking to them from heaven, "Come up here!" They will go up into heaven in a cloud. Their enemies will watch them. [13] At that moment, there will be a great earthquake. Ten percent of the city will fall. 7,000 persons will be killed in the earthquake. The other people will be frightened. They will give glory to the God of heaven.

### God will Rule Forever

[14] The second horror is gone. Listen! The third horror is coming soon.

[15] The seventh angel sounded his trumpet. There were loud voices in heaven. They said, "The kingdom of the world has become the kingdom of our Lord *God* and of His Christ. He will rule forever and ever!" [16] The twenty-four elders were sitting on their thrones in front of God. They fell down on their faces and worshiped God. [17] They said, "We thank you, Lord God, the all-powerful One, the One who is and the One who was. You have used Your great power and have begun to rule. [18] The people of the world were angry, but Your punishment has come. The right time has come to judge people who have died, to give rewards to Your servants, the prophets, to the holy people, and to those who respect Your name—the unimportant people and the important people—and to destroy those people who destroy the earth." [19] God's temple sanctuary was opened in heaven. The holy chest which holds God's agreement appeared in His temple sanctuary. There were flashes of lightning, rumblings, thunder, an earthquake, and large hailstones.

> *The kingdom of the world has become the kingdom of our Lord God and of His Christ.*
>
> *Revelation 11:15*

---

11:11 [c] or, the Spirit of life
11:11 [d] or, enter

## A Woman Gives Birth to a Son

**12** [1] A great sign appeared in heaven. It was of a woman dressed with the sun. The moon was under her feet. A crown of twelve stars was on her head. [2] She was pregnant. Because she was about to give birth and suffer, she cried out in pain.

[3] Then another sign appeared in heaven. Look! It was a large red dragon. It had seven heads and ten horns. Seven crowns were on its seven heads. [4] Its tail dragged one-third of the stars from the sky and threw them toward earth. The dragon stood in front of the woman who was about to give birth. He wanted to eat up the child as soon as it was born. [5] She had a baby boy who would rule all of the people of the world with an iron rod. But her child was taken away to God, to His throne. [6] The woman ran away into the desert.

> *But they have defeated him because of the Lamb's blood and because of the message of their testimony.*
>
> *Revelation 12:11*

She had a place there which God had prepared for her. She could be cared for in that place for 1,260 days.

[7] There was a war in heaven. Michael and his angels fought against the dragon. The dragon and his angels fought back. [8] But the dragon was not strong enough. There was no place left for the dragon and his angels in heaven anymore. [9] The large dragon was thrown out. (This is the old snake who is the same as the one called the Devil, Satan. He is the one who fools the whole world.) He was thrown down to the earth. He and his angels were thrown out. [10] I heard a loud voice in heaven say, "Now have come the salvation, the power, the kingdom of our God, and the authority of His Christ, because the accuser of our brothers has been thrown out. He always accuses them in front of our God day and night. [11] But they have defeated him because of the Lamb's blood and because of the message of their testimony. Even when they were about to die, they did not love their lives *more than God*. [12] This is why you should celebrate, O heavens and those of you who live there. How horrible it will be for the earth and the ocean, because the Devil has come down to where you are. He is very angry. He knows that he only has a short while."

[13] When the dragon saw that he was thrown *down* to the earth, he hunted for the woman who had given birth to the boy. [14] Two wings from a large eagle were given to the woman, so that she could fly to her place in the desert. There, away from the presence of the snake, she would be taken care of for a time, times, and half a time. [15] Behind her the snake vomited

up a lot of water, like a river. He wanted to sweep her away with the flood. ¹⁶But the earth helped the woman. The earth opened up its mouth and swallowed the river of water which the snake had vomited. ¹⁷The dragon was very angry at the woman. The dragon left to make war against the rest of her children. They obey the commands of God and they hold the testimony of Jesus. ¹⁸The dragon stood on the beach.

## The Wild Animal

**13** ¹I saw a wild animal coming up out of the ocean. It had ten horns and seven heads. There were ten crowns on its ten horns. And there was a filthy name on each head. ²The wild animal that I saw looked like a leopard. Its feet were like the feet of a bear, and its mouth was like a lion's mouth. The dragon gave his power, his throne, and his great authority to the wild animal. ³One of its heads seemed as though it had been seriously wounded, but the death wound had been healed. The people of the whole world were so amazed that they followed the wild animal. ⁴They worshiped the dragon, because he gave the wild animal authority. They also worshiped the wild animal, saying, "Who is like the wild animal? Who could fight it?"

⁵It was given a mouth to talk big and say evil things against God. It could use its authority for 42 months. ⁶It opened its mouth to say evil things against God, against God's name, God's tent, and those who live in heaven. ⁷It was allowed to start a war against the holy people and to defeat them. It received authority over every tribe, people, language, and nation, ⁸but not over the people who have their names written in the Lamb's Book of Life. Before the world was created, *God planned for* the Lamb to be killed. All of the other people who are living on earth will worship the wild animal.

⁹If someone has an ear, he should listen:

¹⁰"If anyone is supposed to be captured,
then he will surely be captured.
If anyone is supposed to be killed with a sword,
then he will surely be killed with a sword."

This means that holy people must endure and be faithful.

¹¹I saw another wild animal coming up out of the earth. It had two horns like a lamb's horns. It was talking like a dragon. ¹²On his behalf, it used the complete authority of the wild animal that had already come. It forced the earth and the people there to worship the first wild animal whose death wound had been healed. ¹³It performed great proofs. It made fire come down to earth from the sky in front of human beings. ¹⁴It used

their miracles to fool the people who were living on the earth. These powers had been given to it in the presence of the *first* wild animal. It told the people living on earth to make an idol for the *first* wild animal. (This was the one that had been killed with a sword, but it had come back to life.) ¹⁵ It was allowed to give the breath of life to the wild animal's idol. It talked and forced everyone to worship the idol or to be killed. ¹⁶ It forced everyone to receive a mark on his right hand or upon his forehead— unimportant people and important people, rich and poor, free men and slaves. ¹⁷ No one was allowed to buy or sell, if he didn't have the mark (the wild animal's name or number of the name).

¹⁸ This is *true* wisdom: The person who has understanding should figure out the number of the wild animal. (It is the same way that men count.) Its number is 666.

## Jesus and His People

**14** ¹ I looked and there was a Lamb. He was standing on Mount Zion.ᵃ 144,000 people were with him. They had his name and his Father's name written on their foreheads. ² I heard a sound coming from the sky. It sounded like the roar of much water and like the sound of thunder. The sound I heard was also like the music coming from harps. ³ They were singing a new song in front of the throne, the four beings, and the elders. No one could learn that song—only the 144,000. They had been purchased from the earth. ⁴ They are virgins.ᵇ *Evil* women have not made them *spiritually* unclean. They follow the Lamb wherever he goes. They were bought from among human beings. They are the first ones to be offered to God and to the Lamb. ⁵ They never tell a lie. They are spotless.

## The Time for Judgment

⁶ I saw another angel flying in the middle of the air. He had the eternal Good News to tell those who are living on the earth—every nation, tribe, language, and people. ⁷ He said with a loud voice: "Respect God and give Him glory! The time has come for God to judge. Worship the One who made the sky, the earth, the ocean, and the springs of water!"

⁸ A second angel followed. He said, "It has fallen! The great city of Babylon has fallen!" She had forced all of the nations to drink the punishing wine of her sexual sin.

⁹ A third angel followed the first two angels. He said with a loud voice: "If anyone worships the wild animal and his idol and receives a mark on

---

14:1   ᵃ   Zion was symbolic of the holiest place on earth to the Jews—God's temple in Jerusalem. The temple was built on this mountain. See Micah 4; Isaiah 40; Hebrews 12:22-23.
14:4   ᵇ   They were spiritual virgins. They kept themselves pure, faithful to God.

his forehead or on his hand, [10] he must drink from God's punishing wine. It has been poured full strength into God's cup of punishment. That person will be tortured in front of the holy angels and the Lamb with fire and sulfur. [11] The smoke will rise forever and ever from torturing those who worship the wild animal and its idol or anyone who receives the mark of its name. Day or night they will have no rest *from suffering*."

[12] This means that holy people must endure. They must obey God's commands and hold onto the faith of Jesus.

[13] Then I heard a voice coming from heaven. It said, "Write this: 'From now on, the people who die in the Lord are happy. The Spirit says that they will enjoy rest after they have worked so hard. Their *good* deeds follow them.' "

## Harvest!

[14] I looked and there was a white cloud. There was one sitting on the cloud. He looked like *the* Son of Man.[c] He had a golden crown on his head and a sharp sickle in his hand. [15] Another angel came out of the temple sanctuary. This angel shouted very loudly to the one who was sitting on the cloud, "Send out your sickle! Harvest! The time for the harvesting has come! The earth harvest is ready!" [16] So the one who was sitting on the cloud swung his sickle across the earth and harvested the earth.

[17] Another angel came out of the temple sanctuary in heaven. He had a sharp sickle, too. [18] And another angel came from the altar. He had power over fire. He called loudly to the angel with the sharp sickle, "Send out your sharp sickle! Gather the bunches of grapes in the vineyard of the earth. Its grapes are ripe!" [19] So, the angel swung his sickle to earth and gathered the grapes from the vineyard of the earth. Then he threw them into the winepress of God's anger. [20] Outside the city, the grapes were crushed down in this tank. All around for 180 miles the blood flowed out of the tank. It came up as high as the mouth of a horse!

## The Seven Plagues

**15** [1] I saw another great and amazing warning in heaven: There were seven angels with the last seven plagues. With them God's punishment will be finished.

[2] I saw something which looked like a glass lake mixed with fire. Some people had defeated the wild animal, its idol, and the number of its name. They were standing on this glass lake. They had the harps of God. [3] They were singing the song of Moses, God's servant, and the song of the Lamb:

---

14:14    [c] See Daniel 7:13-14. This refers to Jesus, the Messiah.

"Your actions are great and amazing,
Lord God Almighty.
Your ways are fair and true,
O King of the nations.
[4] Lord, who would not respect You
and give glory to Your name?
Only **You** are holy.
All of the nations will come and
worship before You.
Your righteous deeds have become clear."

[5] Later I saw this: The special tent of the temple sanctuary in heaven was open. [6] The seven angels with the seven plagues came out of the temple sanctuary. They were dressed in clean, bright linen and they wore golden belts around their waists. [7] Then one of the four beings gave the seven angels seven golden bowls of the punishment of God who lives forever and ever. [8] The temple sanctuary was filled with smoke which came from the glory and power of God. No one could go into the temple sanctuary until the seven plagues of the seven angels were finished.

## Sin Is Punished

16 [1] I heard a loud voice coming from the temple sanctuary. It was saying this to the seven angels: "Go and pour out the seven bowls of God's punishment on the earth!"

[2] The first angel left and poured out his bowl on the earth. This caused terrible ugly sores on the people who had the wild animal's mark and who worshiped its idol.

[3] The second angel poured out his bowl in the ocean. The ocean changed into something like the blood of a dead man. Every living thing in the ocean died.

[4] The third angel poured out his bowl in the rivers and springs of water. They changed into blood.

[5] I heard this angel say this:

"You are fair, O Holy One, who is and who was,
because You have decided *to do* these things.
[6] They made *Your* holy people and prophets bleed.
So, You gave them blood to drink.
They deserve this."

[7] I heard someone at the altar say this:

"Yes, Lord God Almighty, Your decisions[a] are true and fair!"

[8] The fourth angel poured out his bowl on the sun. He was allowed to use fire to burn people. [9] They were burned by the intense heat. They said evil things against the name of God, who had the control of these plagues, but they wouldn't change their hearts and give glory to God.

[10] The fifth angel poured out his bowl on the throne of the wild animal. The wild animal's kingdom became dark. Because of the pain, people chewed on their own tongues. [11] They said evil things against the God of heaven, because they had sores and they were in pain. But they wouldn't change their hearts about the *evil* things which they were doing.

[12] The sixth angel poured out his bowl into the great river, Euphrates. The water in it was dried up to prepare the road for the kings of the east. [13] Then I saw three evil spirits that looked like frogs. They came out of the mouths of the dragon, the wild animal, and the false prophets. [14] They are spirits of demons; they perform miracles. They go out to the kings of the whole world, to bring them together for Almighty God's great day of battle.

[15] Listen! I am coming *suddenly*, like a robber. The person who is awake and holds onto his clothes will be happy. He will not walk around naked and be ashamed in front of people. [16] He gathered them to a place called Armageddon in the Hebrew language.

[17] The seventh angel poured out his bowl into the air. A loud voice came from the throne from the temple sanctuary: "It is done!" [18] There were flashes of lightning, rumblings, thunder, and a great earthquake. There has never been such an earthquake since man has been on earth. It was tremendous! [19] The great city broke into three parts. The cities of the people of the world fell down. God did not forget the great city of Babylon; He gave her the wine cup filled with His punishment. [20] Every island disappeared. Even mountains could not be found. [21] Giant hailstones rained down on people from the sky. Each of the hailstones weighed about 100 pounds! Because of the hailstone plague, the people said evil things against God. This plague was awful.

## The Great Whore

**17** [1] One of the seven angels who had the seven bowls came. He spoke with me, "Come, I will show you the condemnation of the famous whore.[a] She sits on much water. [2] The kings of the earth have committed sexual sin with her. The people who live on the earth have gotten drunk from the wine of her sexual sin."

16:7    [a] literally, judgments
17:1    [a] prostitute—a bad woman. She sold her body to men to use for sex.

[3] In the Spirit, the angel carried me away to a desert. I saw a woman sitting on a wild animal. It was red. It had ungodly names written all over it. It had seven heads and ten horns. [4] The woman was dressed in purple and red clothes. She was covered with gold, precious jewels, and pearls. She had a golden cup in her hand. It was full of obscene and filthy things which came from her sexual sin. [5] This name, which has a secret meaning, was written on her forehead:

BABYLON THE GREAT
THE MOTHER OF WHORES
AND
THE FILTHY THINGS OF THE WORLD

[6] I could see that the woman was drunk from the blood of holy people and the blood of Jesus' witnesses.

I was amazed when I saw this great sight. [7] The angel asked me, "Why are you amazed? I will tell you the secret about the woman and the wild animal that she is riding. It has seven heads and ten horns: [8] The wild animal that you saw existed at one time, but does not exist now. It is about to come up out of the bottomless *pit* and go to destruction.[b] There will be people who live on earth whose names have not been written in the Book of Life, since the beginning of the world. They will be amazed when they see the wild animal, because he existed one time. He does not exist now, but he will come back.

[9] "The person who has wisdom will understand this: The seven heads are seven hills. The woman is sitting on them. They are seven kings, too. [10] Five kings have fallen, one king is now ruling, and another king has not yet come. When he does come, he must last for a little while. [11] The wild animal that existed at one time, but does not exist now, is an eighth king. He belongs with the seven kings. He is going off to destruction.[c] [12] The ten horns that you saw are ten kings. They have not yet received their kingdoms. But, along with the wild animal, they will get the power of kings for one hour. [13] They have one goal—they must give their power and authority to the wild animal. [14] They will fight against the Lamb. But the Lamb will defeat them, because he is Lord of lords and King of kings. The people with the Lamb are the called, the chosen and the faithful."

[15] Then the angel said this to me: "The waters that you saw, where the whore sits, are peoples, crowds, nations, and languages. [16] The ten horns and the wild animal that you saw will hate the whore. They will abandon

---

17:8    [b] hell
17:11   [c] hell

her, leaving her naked and ruined. They will eat her flesh and destroy her by fire. ¹⁷ God has put this *desire* into their hearts—to accomplish His purpose and to give their kingdom to the wild animal, until the words of God come true. The woman whom you saw is the great city which has a kingdom *ruling* over kings of the world."

## Babylon Has Fallen

18 ¹ Later I saw another angel coming down from heaven. He had great authority. His glory lighted the earth. ² He shouted this with a strong voice:

"It has fallen! The great city of Babylon has fallen!
She has now become a home for demons
and a place for every evil spirit,
for every spiritually unclean, hated bird.
³ She has forced all of the nations to drink
from the raging wine of her sexual sin.
The kings of the earth committed sexual sin with her.
The businessmen of the earth became rich
from her lust for power."

⁴ I heard another voice coming from heaven. It said:

"Come out of her, my people!
You must not share in her sins!
Get away from the plagues which come upon her!
Don't get caught with her!
⁵ Her sins are piled up all the way to heaven.
God has not forgotten her crimes.
⁶ Treat her as she treated others!
Pay her back double for the *evil* things she did.
She mixed a cup *of suffering* for others;
mix it double for her!

⁷ She gave herself glory and luxury.
Pay her back with torture and pain.
In her heart she boasts,
'I am a queen sitting here.
I am not a widow.
I will never feel pain.'
⁸ This is why plagues will come on her in one day.
There will be death, sorrow, and no food.

Fire will burn her up.
The Lord God is strong; He judges her."

[9] When the kings of the earth see the smoke from her burning, they will cry over her. They had committed sexual sin with her and shared luxury with her. [10] She is being punished. They will be afraid. So they will stand far away, saying, "How horrible this is! How horrible this is for you, O great, strong city of Babylon! Your condemnation came in one hour!"

[11] The businessmen of the earth will cry over her and feel sorry. No one will buy their cargoes anymore: [12] cargoes of gold and silver; of precious jewels and pearls; of fine cotton, purple dye, silk, and scarlet cloth; of all kinds of citron wood, ivory articles, and expensive woods; of brass, iron, and marble; [13] of cinnamon, spice, incense, perfume, and precious spices; of wine and olive oil; of fine flour and wheat; of cattle, sheep, horses, and wagons; and of the bodies and the souls of human beings. [14] All things that you wanted are gone. All of your wealth and glamor have disappeared. No one will ever be able to find them.

[15] The men who did business with these things stood far away. They had gotten rich because of her, but now they were afraid. She was being punished. They were crying and feeling sorry. [16] They said:

"How horrible this is! How horrible this is for you,
O great city!
You were dressed with fine cotton, purple, and scarlet cloth.
You wore gold, precious jewelry, and pearls.
[17] Such wealth was destroyed in only one hour!"

Every ship captain, sea traveler, sailor, and sea merchant stood far away. [18] They saw her going up in smoke. They were shouting, "What city was ever like this city?" [19] They began to throw dust on their heads.[a] They were yelling and feeling sorry. They said:

"How horrible this is! How horrible this is for the
great city!
All those who owned ships in the ocean became
rich because of her.
But, in only one hour, it was all destroyed!
[20] O heaven, celebrate over her!
You, too, holy people, apostles, and prophets,
because God condemned her for the way she treated you."

18:19    [a] This was a way of showing extreme anger.

[21] Then a strong angel lifted up a large stone and threw it into the ocean. (It was the size of a grinding stone.) He said:

"The great city of Babylon will be thrown down
　　with this kind of force.
　　It will never be found again.
[22] The sound of musicians who play the harp, the flute,
　　　and the trumpet
　　will never be heard there again.
Not one of the skills of any kind of worker
　　will ever be found there again.
The sound of a grinding stone
will not be heard there again.
[23] The light from a lamp
　　will never shine there again.
The sound of a bride and groom
　　will never be heard there again.
Your businessmen were very important on earth.
　　The nations were fooled by your tricks of magic.
[24] The blood of prophets, holy people, and everyone on earth who was killed was found in her."

## Praise God!

19 [1] Later, I heard something in heaven. It sounded like the roar of a large crowd. The people were saying:
"Hallelujah![a]
　Salvation, glory, and power belong to our God
　[2] because His decisions[b] are true and fair.
　God has condemned the famous whore
　　who used her sexual sin to spoil the world.
　She killed the servants of God,
　　but He has avenged their blood."
[3] Again they said:
"Hallelujah!
*She is burning and* her smoke will go up forever and ever."
[4] The twenty-four elders and the four beings fell down and worshiped God who was sitting on the throne. They said, "Amen! Hallelujah!"

## They Worship

[5] A voice came out from the throne:

---

19:1　[a]　A Hebrew expression meaning "Praise Yahweh," i.e. "Praise the Lord."
19:2　[b]　literally, judgments

"Let all of God's servants,
    those who respect Him,
    unimportant and important people,
    praise our God."

⁶ Then I heard something like the sound of a large crowd. It was like the roar of lots of water and loud thunder:

"Hallelujah!
    The Lord our God rules.
        He is all-powerful.
⁷ Let us be happy and glad
    and give God the glory,
    because the wedding of the Lamb has come.
    His bride has prepared herself *for him*.

⁸ She was given clean, bright, fine linen to wear." (The fine linen means the good things which holy people did.)

⁹ Then the angel said to me, "Write this down: 'The people who have been invited to the Lamb's wedding are happy.' These are the true words of God."

¹⁰ I fell down at the angel's feet to worship him, but he said to me, "Don't do that! Worship **God**! I am only a servant, like you and your brothers who have the truth that Jesus gave. The truth that Jesus gave is what inspires prophets."

## Jesus

¹¹ I saw heaven opened. Look! There was a white horse! The person who was riding on it was called Faithful and True. He judges fairly. He makes war. ¹² His eyes are like the flame of a fire. There are many crowns on his head. He has a name written on him. He is the only one who knows it. ¹³ He is dressed with a robe dipped in blood. His name is The Message of God. ¹⁴ The armies in heaven are following him on white horses. They are dressed in pure, white, fine linen. ¹⁵ A sharp sword comes out of his mouth. He uses it to hit the nations. **He** will shepherd them with an iron rod. **He** will crush down *the grapes* of Almighty God's angry punishment in the winepress. ¹⁶ He has this name written on his robe and on his thigh:

### KING OF KINGS AND LORD OF LORDS

¹⁷ I saw an angel standing in the sun. He shouted very loudly to all the birds flying around in the middle of the air, "Come, gather at God's great dinner! ¹⁸ You will eat the flesh of kings, of commanders, of strong men, of horses and their riders, of all free men, of slaves, and of unimportant and important people."

[19] Then I saw the wild animal, the kings of the earth, and their armies gathered to fight against the one who was riding the *white* horse and against his army. [20] The false prophet had performed miracles in the presence of the wild animal. The false prophet had used these miracles to fool the people who received the mark of the wild animal and who worshiped the wild animal's idol. But both the wild animal and the false prophet were captured and thrown alive into the fiery lake which burns with sulfur. [21] The one who rode the *white* horse used the sword that came from his mouth to kill the other soldiers. All the birds ate up their flesh.

## The Thousand Years

**20** [1] I saw an angel coming down from heaven. He had a key to the bottomless *pit* and a big chain in his hand. [2] He grabbed the dragon (that old snake, the Devil, Satan) and tied him up for 1,000 years. [3] Then the angel threw him into the bottomless *pit*. Then he shut *the door* and sealed it, so that the dragon could not fool the nations until the 1,000 years were finished. After these things, the dragon must be set free for a short time.

[4] I saw thrones, too. People sat on them. These were the souls of people who had been killed, because they had told the truth about Jesus and because *they had preached* the message of God. They had not worshiped the wild animal or its idol. They had not received the mark upon their foreheads or on their hands. They were given the power to judge. They lived and ruled with Christ for 1,000 years. [5] (The other dead people did not come back to life until the 1,000 years were finished. This is the first rising from death. [6] The person who has a part in this first resurrection is happy and holy. The second death does not have any power over these people. Instead, they will be priests of God and Christ. They will rule with Christ for 1,000 years.)

[7] When the 1,000 years is finished, Satan will be set free from his prison. [8] He will go out in all four directions of the earth to fool the nations—to Gog and Magog[a]—to gather them for war. There will be many, many soldiers. It will be like the number of the grains of sand on the beaches. [9] They will come across the surface of the earth and surround the camp of the holy people and the city which *God* loves, but fire will come down from heaven and burn them up. [10] The Devil who fooled them will be thrown into the lake which burns with sulfur. That is where the

---

20:8    [a] The location is not certain. It may have the spiritual meaning of "all people who are against God." Compare Revelation 11:8; Ezekiel 38:2.

wild animal and the false prophet are. They will be tormented day and night, forever and ever.

## The Judgment Day

[11] And I saw a great white throne and the One who was sitting on it. The earth and the sky ran away from His face, but they could not find any place *to hide.* [12] I saw dead people—important and unimportant. They were standing in front of the throne. Books were opened. And another book—the Book of Life—was opened. The dead were judged from the things which had been written in the books, according to the way they had lived. [13] The ocean yielded the dead people who were in it. Death and Hades[b] yielded the dead people who were in them. Each person was judged by the way he had lived. [14] Death and Hades were thrown into the lake of fire. (The second death is the same thing as the lake of fire.) [15] If someone's name was not found in the Book of Life, he was thrown into the lake of fire.

## The New Jerusalem

**21** [1] Then I saw a new sky and a new earth. The first sky and the first earth were gone. The ocean didn't exist anymore, either. [2] I saw the holy city, the new Jerusalem, coming down out of heaven from God. It was like a bride prepared for her husband-to-be; she was beautiful. [3] And I heard a loud voice coming from the throne. It said, "Look! God's sanctuary[a] is among human beings. God will live with them.

> *And God will wipe away every tear from their eyes. None of these things will exist: death, sorrow, crying, pain.*
>
> *Revelation 21:4*

They will be His people. God Himself will be with them, and He will be their God. [4] And God will wipe away every tear from their eyes. None of these things will exist: death, sorrow, crying, pain. (Old things have passed away.)"

[5] The One who was sitting on the throne said, "Listen, I am making everything new. Write this down, because these words are dependable and true: [6] It is done! I am the A and the Z,[b] the Beginning and the End. From the Spring of Life I will freely give water to the thirsty person. [7] The

---

20:13    [b]   the Greek word for the unseen world of the dead

21:3    [a]   literally, tent

21:6    [b]   literally, the Alpha and the Omega (the first and last letters of the Greek alphabet). Here it means the beginning and the end.

person who is victorious will receive all these things. I will be his God. And, he will be My son. [8] However, people who are cowards, unbelievers, perverts, murderers, sexual sinners, those who follow occult practices, idol-worshipers, and all liars will be in the lake which burns with fire and sulfur. This is the second death."

## The City Walls

[9] One of the seven angels came. (These angels were the ones who had the seven bowls which had been full of the last seven plagues.) He spoke with me, "Come, I will show you the bride of the Lamb." [10] In the Spirit, he carried me to a very tall mountain. He showed me the holy city, Jerusalem. It was coming down out of heaven from God. [11] It had God's glory. It was shining like a very valuable jewel—like crystal-clear jasper. [12] The city had a very high wall, with twelve gates and twelve angels at the gates. Each gate had the name of one tribe of Israel. [13] There were three gates on the east side. There were three gates on the north side. There were three gates on the south side. And, there were three gates on the west side. [14] The wall of the city had twelve foundations. Each foundation had the name of one of the Lamb's apostles.

> *The angel showed me a river of fresh water. It sparkled like crystal. It flowed from God's throne and from the Lamb's throne.*
>
> *Revelation 22:1*

[15] The angel who was speaking to me had a golden measuring stick for measuring the city, its gates, and its wall. [16] The city was square-shaped; its width was the same as its length. The angel measured the city with the stick. The city was 12,000 stadia[c] long. It was 12,000 stadia high and 12,000 stadia wide. [17] The angel measured the wall of the city. It was 144 cubits[d] thick. (The angel was using the same measurement that a man *would use*.) [18] The wall was made of jasper. The city was made of pure gold. (It was like pure glass!) [19] Precious jewels were used to make the foundations of the city walls look more beautiful:

The first foundation jewel was jasper.
The second foundation jewel was sapphire.
The third foundation jewel was chalcedony.
The fourth foundation jewel was emerald.

---

21:16  [c]  About the distance from Rome to Jerusalem. The number is probably a symbol of perfection.
21:17  [d]  About 70 yards. A cubit was about the length of a man's forearm (measuring from the point of the elbow to the tip of the longest finger).

<sup>20</sup> The fifth foundation jewel was onyx.

The sixth foundation jewel was carnelian.

The seventh foundation jewel was yellow quartz.

The eighth foundation jewel was beryl.

The ninth foundation jewel was topaz.

The tenth foundation jewel was chrysoprase.

The eleventh foundation jewel was turquoise.

The twelfth foundation jewel was amethyst.

<sup>21</sup> The twelve gates were twelve pearls. Each gate was made of one pearl. The city's street was made of pure gold, but you could see through it—like pure glass!

<sup>22</sup> I didn't see a temple sanctuary in the city, because the Lord God Almighty and the Lamb are its temple sanctuary! <sup>23</sup> The city had no need for the sun or moon to shine on it—God's glory gives it light and the Lamb is the lamp of the city. <sup>24</sup> The nations use its light to guide them. The kings of the earth add their splendor to it. <sup>25</sup> Its gates will never be shut, because there is no night there. <sup>26</sup> The glory and honor of the nations will be brought into it. <sup>27</sup> Not one unholy thing will enter the city. No person who is perverted will go in. Liars will not get in. The only people who will enter are the ones whose names are written in the Lamb's Book of Life.

**22** <sup>1</sup> The angel showed me a river of fresh water.<sup>a</sup> It sparkled like crystal. It flowed from God's throne and from the Lamb's throne. <sup>2</sup> The Trees of Life were in the middle of the city's street and on both sides of the river. They made fruit twelve times *per year*, producing their fruit once each month. The leaves of this kind of tree were for healing the nations. <sup>3</sup> Nothing that God has condemned will be found there. God's throne and the Lamb's throne will be in the city.

God's servants will worship Him with service. <sup>4</sup> They will **see** God's face! His name will be *written* on their foreheads. <sup>5</sup> There will be no night anymore. They will not need the light from a lamp or the light from the sun, because the Lord God will shine on them. They will rule as kings forever and ever.

### I'm Coming Soon

<sup>6</sup> The angel said to me, "These words are dependable and true: The Lord, the God of the spirits of the prophets, has sent His angel to show

22:1    <sup>a</sup>   or, of living water; of *the* Water of Life

His servants what must soon happen. [7]Listen! I am coming soon. Happy is the person who obeys the words of the prophecy of this book."

[8]I, John, was the one who was hearing and seeing these things. When I heard them and saw them, I fell down at the feet of the angel who was showing me these things. I wanted to worship him, [9]but he said to me, "Don't do that! Worship **God**! I am only a servant like you, like your brothers, and like the people who obey the words of this book. [10]Don't seal the words of the prophecy of this book. The right time is near. [11]Let the person who does wrong continue to do wrong. Let the person with a dirty mind continue to think in a filthy way. Let the person who does right continue to do good things. Let the person who is holy continue to be holy."

[12]Jesus said, "Listen! I am coming soon. The reward I have is with me. I will pay back each person according to the way he lived. [13]I am the A and the Z,[b] the first and the last, the beginning and the end."

[14]The people who wash their robes are happy. They will have the right to *eat from* the Tree of Life and the right to enter the city. [15]But, outside the city, there are wild dogs, occult people, sexual sinners, murderers, idol-worshipers, and every person who always likes to tell a lie.

[16]"I, Jesus, sent my messenger to tell the *seven* congregations the truth about these things. I am the Descendant from the family of David, the bright Morning Star."[c]

[17]The Spirit and the bride are saying, "Come!" Let the person who is listening say, "Come!" Let the person who is thirsty come. Let him take as much of the living water as he wants.

## Don't Change a Word

[18]I am telling the truth to every person who is listening to the words of the prophecy of this book. If anyone adds more words to these words, God will add to him the plagues that are written in this book. [19]And, if anyone takes away from the words of this prophetic book, God will take away that person's share of the Tree of Life and the holy city, which are written about in this book.

[20]The Witness says these things, "Yes, I am coming soon!"

Amen! Lord Jesus, come!

[21]May the gracious love of the Lord Jesus be with everyone.

---

22:13  [b]  literally, the Alpha and the Omega (the first and last letters of the Greek alphabet). Here it means the beginning and the end.

22:16  [c]  Jesus. He brings on a new day.

# ALSO FROM ELMER TOWNS

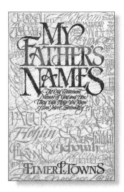

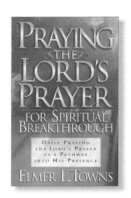
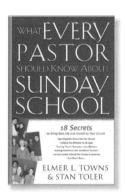
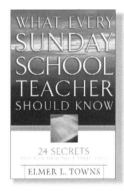

**Praying the Psalms**
To Touch God and
Be Touched by Him
*Elmer Towns*
ISBN: 0-7684-2195-0

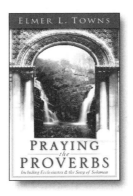

**Praying the Proverbs**
Including Ecclesiastes and
the Song of Solomon
*Elmer Towns*
ISBN: 0-7684-2316-3

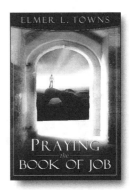

**Praying the Book of Job**
Learning How to Endure
Life's Hardships
*Elmer Towns*
ISBN: 0-7684-2361-9

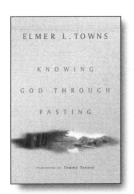

**Knowing God
Through Fasting**
Foreword by Tommy Tenney
*Elmer Towns*
ISBN: 0-7684-2069-5